EAT
DRINK
THINK

RENAE SAAGER

TABLE OF CONTENTS

A LETTER FROM ME TO YOU

So many people downplay their life, their pain, and their experiences. As if there is a competition for who has the worst life—and an assumption that when we have addiction, mental health issues, or just life struggles, it is connected to a traumatic childhood or dark past. I'm here to say that isn't always the case. Eating disorders, alcoholism, anxiety, depression, shitty days—they can and do happen to anyone.

Even to those of us from a lovely childhood with loving parents. Even to those whose life has been quite nice!

I'm one of those people. And the fact that I had a lovely childhood and comfortable life and still managed to wreak havoc everywhere I went and bring chaos to every new situation, made me feel WORSE. I felt like the cards were all laid out for me. I could see the future I wanted; I just had to "act right" and things would be fine. But I couldn't. I couldn't act right. I couldn't go down the path that was laid before me.

I wrote this book hoping that my story will let you know that you aren't the only one who feels what you're feeling. You aren't the only one with dark thoughts, you aren't the only one with behaviors that trouble you, you aren't the only one with those intense fears, and you aren't the only one with those wild dreams.

And I hope this book will help you take your first steps toward knowing that deep in your own bones.

HOW TO READ THIS BOOK

Real quick before we dig in, let me give you a rundown of what's to come. I begin by sharing my personal journey with you. I take you through the highs, lows, and everything in between. For the longest time, I felt like I was insane and alone on a deserted island. That I was the only one who thought this way, felt this way, and lived this way. Realizing I wasn't was what ultimately changed the trajectory of my life. I'm more of the "leave me alone, I'll do it by myself" kinda person. I thought asking for help, sharing my "weak spots," and not operating at one hundred percent were the worst things you could ever admit to; turns out, it was the only way to feel alive—and stay alive.

After my personal story, I share some more specific steps and insights to help you get out of the food, body, and self-confidence tornado you may be swirling around in, and into the "I don't care who knows—my own needs, wants, and happiness are now at the top" attitude that will put you back on solid ground. I'll address things like, why you can't stop eating (no, you aren't broken), why nothing has worked, how to feel without eating, and how the hell to *actually* change.

To get different, we have to DO different. As fun as all the self-help books that you have acquired over the years may feel, nothing changes you quite like making a different choice.

When you read through this book, I hope you'll begin to see, or further solidify the understanding, that there is no "right" way to eat or live. Clinging to the idea that there must be some code you need to crack and then happiness and success will pour out of your eyeballs and you will never have a bad day with food again, is exactly what will leave you fighting with yourself and never feeling like enough.

I hope you see some of yourself in my story. I hope you feel seen, know that I'm here, *getting it*, and understanding you. But beyond that, I want you to be able to take action so that this book isn't just another thing making you feel bad about yourself because you were inspired . . . but made no change in your own life. I want you to take that first step off the exhausting hamster wheel of constantly running from anxiety, micromanaging food and weight, and living according to expectation. So, after my own story, I offer you the most essential insights and mindset shifts that got me off that wheel. I've used them to help client after client step off the wheel too. And there are prompts to help you begin putting this into practice in your own life right away.

Or, like, just enjoy the book for what it is and carry on with your life. That is okay too. Either way, let's do this.

PART 1:

THE TORNADO

INTRODUCTION:
ROCK BOTTOM

"**G**ood luck."

It was 2009 when my mom threw my single duffle bag containing all my belongings into a place I would now call "home." She was done. She was past the point of being mad, she was past the point of feeling anger or using words; she was simply done.

A couple of days before, she had received a call from a woman she hadn't spoken to in years. "Your daughter is here. She is drunk, destroying our home, and I have no idea what to do with her." At that point, I was technically homeless. I had nowhere to go and no one to call. And I hadn't been sober in weeks.

I had just been kicked out of three places due to my drinking. Places with amazing women who

I was initially able to show up sober for and have a conversation with and convince them I was a normal, hard-working person with nothing to hide. But within weeks, I'd be holed up in my room, curtains pulled, phone charger close by, with to-go food containers and vodka bottles carpeting the floor, going between blackout drunk to drinking so I could get back to being blackout drunk.

In the last place I had been renting a room, just after I'd been fired from my job at the Hilton Hotel, my roommate came into my room to check on me because I hadn't been out in days. She found maggots in one of the aforementioned food containers. I do feel awful about the maggots and am equally as grossed out as you are right now. Even though I was a drunk mess of a person, I knew this chick was kind of weird too. I mean, all her furniture was wrapped in plastic sheets. Like it was supposed to be in a showroom but was actually in a living room in a home where people lived. Who does that?! But, in all honesty, that was a pretty great setup for me considering I would frequently pee my pants or involuntarily vomit. She also had two sponges with sticky notes on them so I would know which was for the dishes and which was for the counter. I cannot believe our paths crossed because I know, even stone-cold sober, my antics and "good enough" idea of what clean was must have been this woman's worst nightmare. I can't imagine what experiencing me drunk put her through—I am sure she still thinks about me. With the maggots, the booze, and being fired from yet another job, you may be shocked to hear this—she kicked me out.

With nowhere else to go, I somehow ended up at my mom's old friend's house (I say "somehow" because a lot of my days were a blur, and I have no recollection of getting to new places or even of one day ending and another beginning).

I'm not exactly sure what my mom thought in that moment, coming to pick me up and seeing her daughter unshowered, disheveled, drunk, and stumbling about, but I would imagine it was something like, *This is the last time.* She drove four hours to Portland to rescue her daughter . . . *again.* I do know however that the only reason she came and got me was because she felt sorry for the person's home I was destroying—she made that clear. That woman did not deserve my behavior, and she was too nice to kick me out or call the cops.

My mom's anger was palpable when she arrived, despite my being drunk. Her teeth were clenched, her movements rigid, and eye contact minimal. Normally, I would have felt guilty about putting her out like this, but the great thing about booze is it helps you not feel. So while I saw my mom's anger, I didn't have to feel it—which was exactly why I'd started drinking to begin with. I wanted an escape. To dull out the big emotions.

And after a couple of years of sky-high tolerance, alcohol was still doing the job. Sure, my entire life and all my relationships had gone up in flames, but when you don't feel anything, nothing matters.

The few articles of clothing I had were picked up from inside the home, and we left. She took me to a hotel, and while we were there, she had me start calling "Oxford houses." This is a type of transitional housing where you live with other clean and sober women. We knew about this living arrangement from past attempts at getting sober. We found one, I was accepted in, and before I knew it, there I was coming off the heels of a bender, standing inside my new home with women I didn't know and frankly didn't care to, because all I could think of was lying down.

I guess someone showed me where my room was; I can't remember. My brain was a mess. I felt like I was trapped inside a snow globe that someone was continually shaking. I do know I ended up in one with a visibly used mattress, no sheets, no pillows, no blankets, and collapsed on top of it. I didn't have the energy or ability to worry about where the bed came from or whose it was. I needed to rest my brain, which still felt like it was swimming in vodka.

That was the last time I drank alcohol.

I had been waiting for a magic pill. I had wanted to just snap my fingers and to have everything I was currently struggling with (wrecked cars, ruined relationships, debt, overwhelm, being jobless) go away and for everything I wanted to appear.

Right up until I face-planted onto that disgusting mattress, I couldn't see the point of trying. Life felt too heavy. The tiniest stuff was impossible. When I was drinking, I wanted nothing more than to just keep drinking. I certainly didn't want to extend the effort of getting "sober," nor did it sound like a better alternative to my current situation. I mean, sober at twenty-two? That is basically the end of one's life, right? That's how it felt.

I don't know if I ever really *wanted* to get sober—I loved the feeling of being fucked up and checked out more than I loved the breath I took.

What was it? What happened that late July that was different for me than in all those years past?

For me, *it was losing everything*. It was losing everything coupled with a handful of days not drinking so I could kind of come back to the "real Renae."

I realized nobody else was going to fix me; I had to do it myself.

So there I was. A single bag of belongings, sleeping on some rando's mattress, and in a new "home" with eight or so strangers, still so hungover I couldn't stand up while showering—trying to think about how the hell I was going to do this.

After a couple of days, I was finally sober enough to have a little food and get dressed. And after a couple of weeks, I regained some clarity and my ability to think straight.

But with that clarity, the real problem returned. So, let's go back to the beginning . . .

CHAPTER 1:
SLOW BURN

With all the chaos and drinking I did, there must have been a good reason, right? Maybe a sad childhood story? A traumatic event? Something major happened that I had been shoving deep down into my psyche for my entire life? I felt like that was what every therapist and rehab I went to was trying to pull out of me.

Nope. Not in the least. And honestly, that kind of made me feel worse about everything I was doing. My life was being served to me on a silver platter, and I just kept throwing it away. My childhood was great—and that is a big reason I had so many thoughts like *What is wrong with me? Why am I doing this to myself? Do I have a personal vendetta against myself?* Because it certainly felt like it. I felt like two people constantly at war with one another. And let me tell you, when you are in a war with yourself, that is exhausting! Because you never get a break. No matter how many moves you make, jobs you take, relationships you get into, or things you do to stay busy, there you are.

It feels more justified to struggle with addiction when the cards have been stacked against you; when you have a royal flush though—come on—it just doesn't make sense. There is no valid excuse or reason for my feelings and behavior.

Growing up I had two loving parents and one older sibling, Randy. We lived in a small town, where everyone knew everything about everyone all the time. Maybe you are familiar with the type.

- Peggy Sue and Joe Bob got divorced? Obviously it was the topic of lunch conversation with the ladies.
- The word got out that Omar was gay—"But how?! His parents are so loving and levelheaded! MUST DISCUSS IN GREAT DETAIL." Yes, massive eyeroll.
- There was "the bar" where everyone went to.
- And when the first stoplight went in, WHOA. Big-city vibes and lots of talk about "where is this town really headed?"

Every Sunday, we had breakfast out with my grandma and grandpa. We went to the local restaurant where my grandma kept her orange marmalade in the fridge, which was retrieved for her when the server saw us park, and there was rarely a need to actually order because "the usual" was enough.

Those Sunday breakfasts were a big to-do as a kid. All the uncles, cousins, and grandkids came, sometimes twelve or more of us at one table. I loved the big family feel. I loved getting to eat my sausage links and toast with my cousin and the times my grandpa would pour a disgusting amount of cream and sugar into the last of his coffee for me to have a sip, which never happened without hearing, "You know, coffee will stunt your growth."

Those early morning breakfasts were similar to our holidays. Easter, Thanksgiving, Christmas, Fourth of July, etc., we all got together at the designated host's house and the parents drank their wine while the kids ran around.

Holidays were such a magical time in our home as a kid. My mom went above and beyond to make them feel special, and I mean EVERY holiday. These are the things you never fully appreciate until you are an adult. The hours of thought, preparation, and cleanup that must have gone in to every Easter egg hunt, the all-green-everything St. Patrick's Day meal, the Fourth of July barbecue with friends, the pumpkin carving party—with themed foods, of course—a full house for Thanksgiving with all the fixings, and a magical Christmas wonderland with lights everywhere.

You never appreciate all the work that goes into making the holidays special as a child. It just magically appears and you love it, then it magically disappears and you forget about it. But now, I look back with awe, admiration, and love.

(So if you are a parent working your butt off to make your child's holiday experiences special, I promise it is making a greater impact than you know. Your effort isn't fruitless.)

I had all kinds of hobbies growing up and did a terrible job finishing them (some things never change). With each new passion came praise and encouragement. "You've really got an eye for that!" "You know, you could turn this into a career if you really love it." Whether that was tumbling rocks, beading, soccer, or writing.

As far as I'm concerned, my parents were as good as they come. Were they perfect? No. Of course not. But I have no idea what it feels like to go unloved or unhugged as a child.

So why the hell did someone with such a beautiful upbringing need to escape? GREAT QUESTION!

Despite the love, the connection, the holidays, and traditions, why was I living like a stressed out lizard in the desert, darting from thing to thing, always on edge, and certain everyone around me was going to leave or die?

From what my mom has told me, I was stubborn, sassy, and did not want to be held or rocked. I wanted to do things on my own.

While I never wanted my parents too close, I also never wanted them to be too far. Both of my parents were in the dental field, and a couple times a year they would take work trips lasting up to a week, which was the first time I noticed my anxiety. Of course, at the time I had no clue what it was. I was just sure they were going to die, or I was going to die, or something else horrific would happen. And there was no escaping it. The worry started days and even weeks before their trip. I felt like a dog watching its owner pulling out the suitcase, knowing that something was happening and also knowing wherever they were headed, my ticket was not included.

As they got ready to leave the house, I went into total meltdown mode. I clawed at the walls and begged them not to go. I was inconsolable. I cried for hours. My brother, on the other hand, couldn't have cared less. He was either reading or playing a video game, and I'm not sure he was even aware they left.

My fear of being left alone started here, but it was only just beginning.

I had a ride-or-die BFF, Sara, and we talked every single day. We had all the BFF swag, you know, the heart-shaped necklaces, anklets that had "best" on one part and "friend" on the other, and really whatever else Claire's had out on display. We matched our outfits and pulled as many strings as possible to make sure we had all the same classes and always sat next to each other and were overall inseparable.

We would rollerblade for hours around town, grabbing a pizza pocket and Italian soda, and go until nightfall. Just about every weekend, we spent the night at one or the other of our houses watching *TGIF* on Friday, excitedly waiting to see what kind of drama Cory and Topanga were up to while talking about a cute boy from class, a new way to curl our hair, and about our epic day rollerblading. Our families even vacationed together. One of the most fun vacations I went on as a kid was the week-long houseboat trip our families took. Two families, five kids, living in one room on water for a week—and it was amazing. Every day was filled with boating, tanning, eating, and so much laughter.

Sara was the rock I leaned on in my life, and I never realized how much I relied on her—until it started to crumble.

As we got a little older—about ten—I felt something between us shift.

A wave of coldness came from her from time to time, and it would throw me off because it came, for me, completely out of left field. But then, a day or two later, the chill thawed and things would be back to normal.

I tried to brush it off, I told myself I must have been making it up, but I couldn't shake that something was different. I could sense an undercurrent of . . . *something.* I would lightly bring it up to her as we were rollerblading or hanging out after school. "Hey, are we okay?" And she always brushed it off, "Of course!" or "Oh my gosh, Renae, we are always together! We are fine."

I brought it up with my mom and she would console me and offer me a loving and supportive perspective, and I would decide things were fine.

But my gut was right. Things weren't fine.

Since we did everything together, we were of course on the same basketball team. Granted, our town was so small there was really only one option. For years we would ride to events and practices together, and there was this unspoken rule that we were always partners. But one particular night, it was like I didn't even exist. She knew I was there but looked right through me. And, in fact, she went out of her way to make sure I knew we wouldn't be partners that day, calling out her new partner's name loudly for all to hear.

What is happening? I thought. *Why is this happening? Did I do something? I don't understand.*

On that night, I had no partner—and discovered I had no friend.

The person I'd spent most of my life with tossed me aside like an old stuffed animal she'd outgrown. I had noticed some distance growing between us before this night, but this pushed my suspicion over the edge. Even though weeks and months prior, I had tried to play it cool and made up reasons why I wasn't being invited over as frequently or given a hug when I arrived at school any longer.

That night, I was left to scramble around and find a different partner while I watched her and her new friend run the drills, high five, and hold hands. I felt hollow. I watched them hug at the end of the evening while I gathered my stuff and got into my mom's car.

Then the tears hit. I was crying the kind of cry that doesn't let you breathe. I was so confused, so hurt, and so lost. "I don't get it, Mom. Why is she doing this? Why is she like this? What did I do?" After my mom cradled me tight until I could finally breathe and talk coherently, I called my friend.

"Sara . . . (the tears started all over again, just as intense as before) are we still friends?"

She laughed a little as I was hysterically crying on the other end of the phone. "Yeah, of course . . . why?"

What do you mean, WHY? I thought. We'd been doing this whole life thing together, and now I was like an annoying younger sister she was embarrassed to acknowledge in public. "Well, you haven't been including me as much, you didn't pick me to be your partner tonight, and it seems like you don't really like me now."

"Of course, I do! You are still my best friend, Renae. I promise."

I guess I am overreacting? I thought after we hung up.

Her words felt dismissive and I felt crazy for even thinking such a thing, and it was solidified by her response, "Of course . . . I promise . . ."

Over the next four years, Sara plucked me from our primary social situations with surgical precision. And as I tried befriending others, something odd started to happen. These new friends I started spending time with would say something like, "Did you say this about me? Sara told me you did." Or, "Sara told me you thought this about me" (or some other gossip thing for an early teen). But what they were saying was news to me. "I never said that," I would reply, but I could sense the skepticism.

If I told Sara I thought a boy was cute, she suddenly developed a crush on him as well. I felt as though she had a personal vendetta against my happiness. My social life was slipping through my fingers, totally against my will and out of my control.

As an adult reading this, I can see where you might think, "Yeah, kids are kids." But when you are twelve, you do not have the capacity, insight, or tools to analyze these actions and emotions.

This kind of behavior continued for years. Sara held slumber parties that I never got the invite to. Weekend events no longer included me.

Year after year of that social anxiety eroded any trust I had in myself and in how I saw every situation. I feared there was something seriously wrong with me. Questioning the kind of friend I was became all-consuming. *Why don't people want to spend time with me anymore? What is happening?* I couldn't understand what I had done to deserve such treatment. As the connection to other girls in my class started dropping off, I found myself more and more isolated. So when I saw Sara and whoever her new BFF of the week was, dressed in matching clothes they had likely planned on the phone the night before like we used to do, I did the best thing I could as an early teen to soften that sadness.

I reached for the easiest, clearest thing right in front of me: food and my body. I realized focusing on food, exercise, and my body was a blissful distraction from what was going on in my social life. It quieted all the anxiety. Instead of feeling the sadness, I could just not feel anything at all.

Food and exercise quickly became my mechanism for not feeling anything. But that solution came with a huge price tag.

TWO WORDS: KATE MOSS

Early teens. What a god-awful time, amiright? I had started my period, and my body was changing—and of course I became aware of what other girls' bodies looked like and of the boys noticing those other girls' bodies. I paid close attention and discovered which bodies boys liked—and what it took to gain a boy's attention.

Two words: Kate Moss.

Thin, feminine, fragile. Bonus points if you were extra ditzy. I was none of these things.

My mom used to say, "You're just big-boned," and, "You have hips like your mama. I've never been petite." I know she meant well with all the things she said to try and make me feel better when I'd comment about how my thighs touched or how my arms were bigger than other girls'. But they never helped and further confirmed I didn't look like the beautiful girls I saw.

For my entire life, my dad has been health conscious, and my mom was always on a diet.

Every morning, dad would sit in his green lazy boy in the living room, reading the paper. And at the same time each morning, he'd get up and make his smoothie. Drops of this, scoops of that, a splash of this, followed by a harsh blending to 6:00 a.m. ears—et voilà! A dark teal-colored smoothie filled with every single vitamin known to improve one's health and make you live forever.

I started learning about nutrition from magazines and online calorie calculators. My brain was hooked. I spent more time alone due to my dwindled friendships, while my interest in "health"—or, more accurately, "how to make yourself smaller"—ballooned. My dad worked out almost every night in the home gym in our basement. Fitness magazines decorated many of the surfaces, and my mom was often talking about being on a new diet or desperately needing to lose weight.

At this time, I was active in sports, so paying more attention to what I ate and how I worked out wasn't that big of a leap considering my lifestyle and home environment. It wasn't like I woke up one morning and did a one-eighty; it was more of a slow and steady transition.

I started going for short runs around our neighborhood and downstairs on the treadmill. I knew it burned calories and I knew it would make me better at soccer, so why not?

It was fun. In fact, it was a reprieve! It was a reprieve from sitting alone worrying about my social life, and it gave me something to focus on. But with my increase in exercise came an increased interest in nutrition.

It started with articles in *Oxygen* and *Shape* magazines about what to eat for a "lean" body and how important it was to limit carbs and always get enough protein.

"Eat this not that."

"Healthy options at fast-food restaurants."

"How to stay on track when you travel."

I listened, I studied, and I learned more and more. I was hooked. I couldn't get hooked on math or biology, and I couldn't care less about social studies, but the calories in grapes, chicken, sandwiches, and anything else I was eating—SIGN ME UP!

And wouldn't you know—I was pretty damn good at it!

It wasn't long before I knew the calories in pretty much anything: fruits, veggies, different cuts of meat, and the lowest calorie options in any nearby restaurant. My mom was always on a diet, and instead of referring to one of her countless books that was going to be the thing to make her lose the thirty-five pounds on her belly that she often commented on, she would ask me, "What are the calories in that item?"

Since I was turning into an expert on eating the bare minimum and knowing what were the "healthy" options, I decided to join my mom on one of her diets for moral support. I was already beginning to obsess about my food and "health," so it would be an easy thing for me—and why not help my mom out? I knew how much my mom wanted to lose weight, and I figured it would help me stay more diligent and lose weight myself, so it was like a win-win.

My willpower around food and my dedication to exercise was at an all-time high, and I wore it like a badge. Not a single calorie passed my lips that I didn't look up and track. Refusing food made me feel superior in a way, like, "Ha, look at you. You have to eat breakfast. You are so weak. I can go for hours without eating ANYTHING." I felt this sort of tunnel vision developing. I cared less and less about everything and solely focused on the scale, my stomach, and running.

As my relationships at school became more distant and Sara continued her campaign to keep me on the outside, I decided being alone was better. I started challenging myself downstairs on the treadmill while watching Rachael Ray's *30 Minute Meals* on my dad's little ten-inch TV, running farther than I did the day before.

Seventeen minutes. Twenty-five minutes. Thirty-four minutes!

Running became my escape. My escape from no longer having friends at school; my escape from the growing tension between my parents at home; and my escape from the running stream of anxiety I felt bound in every day.

As a fifteen-year-old, my body was extremely receptive to the exercise and food changes. As my body changed, it didn't take long for the comments and compliments to begin rolling in—and I'd be lying if I said I didn't absolutely love them. I felt so strong, confident, and in control. While other people sat around and ate pizza and breadsticks, I ordered the large salad with extra veggies, no cheese, and a vinaigrette on the side. I would hear people talking about how much they hated their body and "shouldn't" be eating something or about their disdain for their current body, and I thought, *I never want that. I never want to feel like that and I won't.*

I grew more interested in cooking. I was watching the Food Network 24/7, reading food and fitness magazines, and frequently looking up the healthiest meal options for developing abs, and I wanted to start preparing my own food. I scoured recipes, looking for something healthy, veggie heavy, but also *good*. I knew how unhealthy restaurants were from the magazine articles, so it was safer for me to cook at home and control everything that went into the dish.

With anything you practice—you get better.

And I got extremely good at cooking. I wasn't cooking just any old meal, I was making lavish feasts: poached cod with roasted tomatoes and polenta; beef Wellington with asparagus; Thai curry and lettuce wraps. And always a heavy side of vegetables.

My parents loved it. I started helping my mom with the meal prep for dinner parties she had. My dad talked me up at work to his staff, raving about how great the meal was. My ability to cook was a hot conversation topic.

I actually felt joy.

I felt proud.

I felt excited.

I felt a purpose.

I felt . . . obsession.

It didn't take long for the fun to wear off and the "HAVE TO" to take hold. There wasn't a clear day that it happened; there wasn't this line I crossed. The thing with eating disorders, or disordered eating as some feel more comfortable calling it, is that it's a spectrum. It's not a "you have it; you don't" kind of thing. It doesn't happen overnight—and conversely, it doesn't just go away either. It was a slow burn.

My obsession with fitness and nutrition was my first binge. I later learned that watching food shows, reading cookbooks, thinking about food, and wanting to control everything I ate were all common behaviors for someone with an eating disorder, or for someone who is restricted or deprived of food.

I began waking up and running before school because I couldn't risk getting busy; I couldn't take the chance that something might come up to prevent me going for my run. I'd worry that I might lose steam midday and not do it if I didn't do it first thing. I slept in my sports bra so I had one less thing to distract me from getting it done.

I switched my creamer to sugar-free and began saying things like, "I just don't feel hungry in the mornings anymore," or, "I had a big lunch, I'll just skip dinner." During lunches at school, I went from bread bowls and full subs to salads, on to just a cup of soup, then to skipping lunch altogether. I wasn't even skipping meals because I thought I was fat at that point; it was a challenge. A game. A competition against myself. Every morning when I woke up, I felt as if I were stepping into a virtual reality game. The game was to go as hard as possible from the second my eyes opened and to eat the least amount possible, work out the most possible, and stay as busy as possible.

The euphoria unleashed by each grueling workout and every skipped meal electrified me, filling me with a profound sense of purpose and achievement. I took the pain and discomfort as a sign I was doing something well and making progress. Progress toward what, I'm not sure, but I knew not working on something felt like the biggest character defect of all time. Not having a goal, not being busy, not working toward something was a waste. I didn't want movies or lazy Saturdays. I wanted to burn calories.

My weight was decreasing, my emotions were unpredictable, and my anxiety was back in full force, no longer calmed by my focus on food and exercise. My mom started to wonder if I had an eating disorder. She noticed some of my peculiar eating habits like switching from regular salad dressing to just balsamic vinegar, always saying I wasn't hungry, needing to control cooking my own food, and doing a rigorous ab routine every single night in my room. My dad chalked it up to me just being a teen. Anytime they brought it up: "Hey, sweetie, how's school?" or "Did you eat lunch today? Are you sure you don't want more?" I brushed it off or tried removing myself from the conversation as quickly as possible.

The comments started at school; those were harder to run from though. At tennis practice one day, the punishment for the losing side was to lie on the court and sizzle like bacon. As I was on the ground in my tennis skirt, wearing a sweatshirt in the middle of summer because I was perpetually cold and aware of how thin my body was, the tennis teacher yelled out, "Well, we all know who really has no fat to lose," looking at me. Or in history class after Thanksgiving break, the teacher, while standing at the podium in front of the class said, "How was everyone's Thanksgiving? How was yours, Renae? Did you gain an ounce or two?" He laughed at his comment along with the rest of the class. Or Sara making a scene at soccer practice in front of the other girls by loudly asking, "So what did YOU eat today, Renae?"

All this was more of a reason to not be around anyone else. I just wanted to be left alone to exercise and cook.

But here's the thing about the body, you can only starve it for so long. Eventually, your hunger breaks through, and you eat or you die. That's pretty much it.

Eventually, my hunger won—thankfully—but my awareness and appreciation for that wouldn't sink in until about fifteen years down the road.

My attention to food—a.k.a. my neurosis around 1 teaspoon of butter vs. 2 or 4 ounces of chicken vs. 4.5—also bled into my appearance. My image at school was on point: my outfits matched and I took care of my appearance and it needed to look great. And when it didn't, cue a COMPLETE MELTDOWN in my bedroom. Bless my mom's heart—trying to console her fifteen-year-old daughter because her jeans felt weird or her gnarly cowlick was acting up. "Renae—it's fine! It isn't a big deal. You look great!"

"NO I DON'T, MOM!!! And you know I don't. I look stupid and just UGH!!" I'd get out through the tears and gasps of air.

What other people thought of me was rapidly becoming more important. As my attitude to food became more unyielding, it did in other areas of my life as well. I wanted everything to be perfect and planned. My tennis game was getting stronger, my runs were getting longer, my calories lower, and my grades were—well, hanging in there!

For as long as I can remember, school was hard for me and I hated it. I remember in second grade staying after class with Mrs. Hendricks as she tried to help me read. I got tested for learning disabilities, had tutors, and my mom would drive me to a place an hour away once or twice a week to get additional support.

I would spend many a night crying over math problems. I would spend hours studying for science exams, making countless flashcards and notes, only to scrape by with a B-minus or C. Embarrassed, I'd hide my grade from the other students, staying after class to try to understand why I got so many questions wrong and what the right answer was. Meanwhile, I saw other students in the class who barely stayed awake during the lecture, or rarely bothered to show up at all, receive the same grade as me. In fact, one kid would rarely ever show up, and when he did he was obviously high and he got an A on every single exam!

Why am I the only one struggling this much? What is wrong with me? I'd think.

I started caring less about school, as it never really clicked for me; instead, I found interest in things I was better at. Like perfecting a cookie recipe, knowing the nutrition information on every restaurant item within a twenty-five-mile radius of home, or forcing myself to run—no matter what. School only got harder and more frustrating, but I got better and better at mastering my full-time job of food and body.

And as if it wasn't bad enough comparing myself to other students at school, it was worse at home. I was the complete opposite of my brother; he is one of those naturally smart people. You know the type.

Not only was he smart, he was also very laid back. By the time he got out of bed around 10:00 or 11:00 a.m., grabbed the box of donut holes from the kitchen, and plopped on the couch in front of *Wheel of Fortune*, I'd already run four miles, showered, baked an elaborate dessert I would never eat, was on my fifth set of crunches, and high on caffeine.

Not only was he smart and relaxed, but to rub the salt in, he had great friends. They just hung out. It all looked so easy for them. So natural.

Seeing him do nothing stressed me out, so I thought doing more could somehow balance that! I thought he was lazy (okay, he really was) but also—and this is the truth that really hurt—he was okay being with himself.

I was not.

My days were always structured:

5:45 a.m.: Wake up and work out

6:45 a.m.: Shower

7:30 a.m.: School

11:30 a.m.: Home to run

12:15 p.m.: Back to school

3:30–5:00 p.m.: Soccer or tennis practice

6:00 p.m.: Family dinner

7:00 p.m.: Read fitness/food magazines

8:00 p.m.: Ab routine

8:30 p.m.: Plan the next day in my journal. Write out the number of calories I'd consumed and calculate, recalculate, then recalculate what I ate that day and different ways I could eat for tomorrow to hit a number I felt good about.

9:00 p.m.: Sleep

It felt like a nice deep exhale, planning this strict schedule each night. But the next day, while I was in the middle of it, I felt like I never actually took a breath. I sucked it in, literally—I remained tense, and I was only focused on the next thing on my to-do list.

My anxiety started building on my anxiety, becoming even more a part of my identity. I had created this idea of who I was and how I presented myself to the world, and even if I didn't like it, I didn't know how to stop. It was like I was on a ride I couldn't get off. Just go, do, and keep moving!

I earned the title "the healthy one." The "fit one."

Restaurants were chosen based on "what Renae would eat." There had to be a salad on the menu, and whatever I ordered I'd sub out any carbs for extra veggies. I planned ahead for every meal. I meticulously studied the nutrition charts. I ate as little as possible when someone else prepared food because I just never knew what they were actually putting on or in the meal.

And in the meantime, at home, things were getting tough. My dad was gone a lot during the evenings for a new art class, scuba diving lessons, a wine tasting lecture, a cooking class, working late—who knows. And that left me and my mom at home.

Her drinking had increased and I was annoyed. Annoyed not just by the drinking, although that didn't help, but by *her*. Simply hearing her breathe made me see red. Hearing her walk through the house, how loudly she put away the dishes, being in the car with her—it didn't matter. Something about my mom's presence in my early teens made me want to rip off my skin.

I thought she just needed to get it together, but in hindsight and with adult eyes, I see what was really happening. My mom's marriage was ending and she knew it; her first-born had left for college, and her daughter was killing herself through starvation and couldn't stand to be in the same room as her. And now, thinking back, I wish I'd crawled into her bed and hugged her and said, "It's okay, Mom. I am still here and I love you." Because she needed that more than anything. But I didn't do that. I thought she was being ridiculous, and right then I couldn't tolerate spending more than five minutes with either parent. Booze was the best she could do for herself.

Something I would come to understand deeply.

CHAPTER 2:
EVERYTHING IN, EVERYTHING OUT

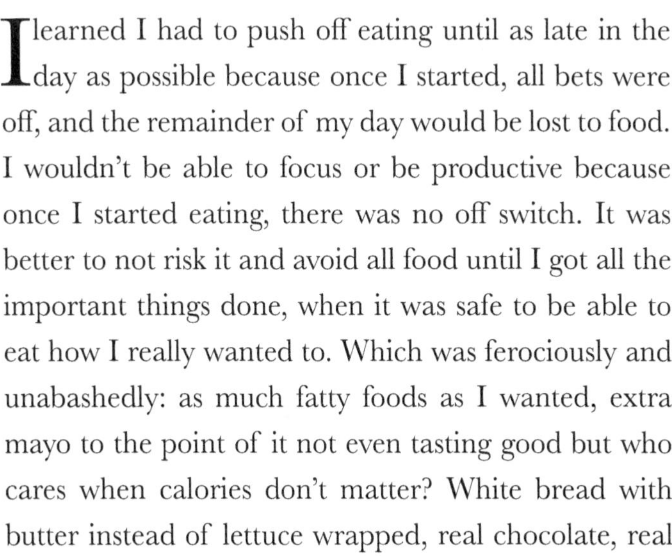

I learned I had to push off eating until as late in the day as possible because once I started, all bets were off, and the remainder of my day would be lost to food. I wouldn't be able to focus or be productive because once I started eating, there was no off switch. It was better to not risk it and avoid all food until I got all the important things done, when it was safe to be able to eat how I really wanted to. Which was ferociously and unabashedly: as much fatty foods as I wanted, extra mayo to the point of it not even tasting good but who cares when calories don't matter? White bread with butter instead of lettuce wrapped, real chocolate, real ice cream with globs of peanut butter added in—all the food I had been indoctrinated to believe one must be careful around and limit.

What everyone around me didn't know and couldn't see was what happened to me in the evenings. As a child (even though fifteen is still a child) I knew how to listen to my body—to rest when I was tired, to stop eating when I was full—but I'd been suffocating those innate cues for so long that when my body told me something now, I didn't care. If it wasn't matching up with what I wanted, I didn't listen. My body became my enemy. It was something I wanted to silence and escape from. I stayed as busy as I could, zipping from one thing to the next; I did crunches to avoid snacking; I chewed gum and drank zero-calorie beverages to try and fill myself up. I went to great lengths to avoid being still or being alone with myself.

I pulled back from almost all social relationships. Even though I desperately wanted human connection, if I was invited to something, I said I was studying, didn't feel well, or some other excuse. When you aren't around, are always busy, or frequently decline invitations, eventually you stop being asked altogether.

When night fell, everything slowed around me. There was no more running around and distracting— just stillness. And I didn't know how to cope. I had hated nighttime since I was a small child. First because that was when my parents left for the dental meetings, and now because I knew it was when the eating would commence. I had learned to put off eating for the night, because I knew once I started, there was no off switch, but also if I didn't eat during the day, I didn't have to feel as much guilt about what I ate at night.

At first, my binge eating was with healthy foods: whole heads of iceberg lettuce dipped in low-calorie dressing, bags of baby carrots, mountains of stir-fried veggies, low-carb tortillas, turkey, low-calorie bread, and sugar-free puddings and Jello. I needed quantity. I wasn't feeding hunger—okay, I absolutely was, because I was essentially starving—but it was deeper than that. I was filling a void. A black hole inside me.

I anxiously awaited my family going to bed because that meant the eating could begin. Any time one of them lingered, I could feel the rage boiling up inside me. "GO TO BED ALREADY!!!" I would have to resist screaming.

The second I knew it was safe, it was game on.

It didn't take long for me to switch from the healthy food that, yes, left me feeling extremely full and massively gassy, to all the carbs I could get my hands on—literally. I ate handfuls of raisin bran until my mouth hurt. I dug out the inside of a loaf of French bread and slathered it in margarine—hiding the rest in the bottom of the garbage can. I revisited what we had for dinner, having a complete second meal. I swallowed it cold and in a crouched position, often using my bare hands.

When I would eat, everything got quiet. When I would eat, it was an escape from everything that bothered me during the day, and I had a moment of my life where everything felt okay. It shut my brain off.

Unfortunately, my nightly eating took on a life of its own I never could have expected.

Over the course of an hour or two, multiple trips to the kitchen, a handful of that, a pinch of this, a spoonful of something else, and I had eaten so much food I could barely breathe. From a slightly hunched over position, because standing straight up put too much pressure on my stomach and back due to all the contents in my stomach, I would tell my mom, "I think something is wrong with me. I cannot stop eating. Once I start eating it's like this monster inside me takes over and I just can't stop. I eat so much food I'm worried my stomach is going to rip."

To which my mom would respond, "Renae, that's good! You need to be eating!"

My weight was now in double digits, and she was absolutely right that eating was what I needed—but she didn't fully understand what I was saying to her. This wasn't just eating. This was out of control. It wasn't me; it was almost like a blackout. It wasn't just the food

I was eating that scared me, it was *how* I felt while I was eating it. But I couldn't stop.

Over time, I mastered my nightly eating routine. At first I was scared of it, but now I had a plan and a routine. I knew which foods made the most noise to open, I knew how to throw away the wrappers and boxes so no one would see the evidence in the morning, I knew where the floors creaked and which cupboard doors made the most noise. I was always on high alert, listening for footsteps that might catch me in the middle of a binge.

And every morning like clockwork, I would wake up, still full from the copious amounts of food I had the night before, roll out of bed, vow today will be different, and go downstairs to the treadmill.

If you keep eating like that, you deserve to be punished. And I would attempt to run off last night's guilt.

Those eating frenzies that left me hunched over in pain, barely making it to my room to collapse, lasted for months . . . close to a year, actually, and increased in length of time and amount of food eaten. Which I didn't think was possible.

One night, it was late—everyone was in bed, and I was hitting all the usuals. Cereal, bread, chocolate, leftovers, a few bites of ice cream, some chips . . . but toward the end I'd eaten so much I thought I was going to be sick. Which wasn't at all unusual because

I typically felt sick, but this was different. I was so painfully full, but I could not stop. The food was up to my throat.

I wasn't even enjoying it at that point, but I couldn't stop eating.

I walked into the bathroom. Lifted the toilet lid. And for the first time in my life, I intentionally threw up.

"Oh. Shit."

I very distinctly remember crossing a line.

Restricting, compulsive exercise, hoarding food, obsessively counting calories, crunches in the middle of the night, nightly binge-eating episodes . . . all that seemed "okay." But throwing up? THAT was not. THAT was something serious.

Shit just got real.

I was overwhelmed with fear and trying to comprehend what happened in that moment—yet I was also flooded with relief. The pain in my stomach was gone, the pressure in my gut was gone, my stomach wasn't so distended that I looked nine months pregnant, and I could fully stand up straight. *Did I just stumble upon the secret to the universe? Is this really how people do it? Is this how you have your cake and eat it too?*

I thought I had a double life before, but it was only just beginning.

THE OBLIVION OF BULIMIA

From that first time I purged for almost the next fifteen years of my life, bulimia consumed me. Thinking back to that time, I would have considered myself a violent bulimic because my eating felt violent—and I was completely out of control. I was still extremely underweight, so I needed to eat a lot of food to get my body and health back in balance, but every time I ate a lot of food, I threw up. And then every time I threw up, I got hungry. Not just hungry but ravenous. Within an hour of throwing up what I had just rapidly inhaled, I would be lightheaded and shaky, I would feel a hollow pit in my stomach needing and wanting food but scared to eat because I didn't want the same cycle to take place. I would tell myself, *It's okay, Renae. Just eat. This is fine. You can eat this.* And I would try. I would make a "normal" looking meal, sit down to eat it, but the cycle would continue. The thing about bulimia is that the whole act is such a fucking rush, which fed right into my personality type. It's an instant escape from life even if it throws you into another type of hell. The dopamine chase was a thrill ride I didn't want to get off; even though at the end of a severe binge-purge episode I was anything but excited, I couldn't stop.

Bulimia became my best friend, or maybe my secret lover.

The food, the bingeing—it made everything quiet in a way that just controlling my food as I did at first no longer could. The eating, the taxing process of purging—it depleted me. I would frequently purge upward of ten times a day. I maintained this secret life for almost fifteen years. In the beginning, I thought I'd found the answer to all my social and anxiety problems. I really thought, *Now I don't need anyone!* But it quickly stopped being optional and became required. In the same way that you wake up and go to pee or cover your mouth when you sneeze—without thinking—I felt like I had to binge and purge to live. It had a choke hold on my life..

When I was sixteen, my parents were worried enough that they thought I should go to therapy and found someone for me to see. I was tired of the energy and effort required to maintain my bulimia; unless it was a "good day," then I totally thought I had it under control and didn't even have a problem. But on the bad days, everything felt completely unmanageable. I would be exhausted, my throat raw. I caved. I agreed to start going to therapy.

So weekly, I sat in an office with a woman who always seemed a bit scattered, drank copious amounts of diet Coke from a large Styrofoam cup, one of those thirty-two-ounce ones you would get from a gas station, and honestly I wondered how "normal" this persons relationship to food was.

Because "we" (people with food and body stuff) all know you drink diet Coke and caffeine like a psycho so you don't eat as much.

I always heard people talk about therapy in such a positive way.

How they loved therapy; how it changed their life; how they had been in therapy for years. And, well, I just never had that experience. I don't know if I ever left therapy thinking, *Wow, that really helped.* Maybe you are a therapist or have been in therapy and love it, and if so, this isn't a dig at you, and also I wish I could have had that kind of experience. I mean, I understand that therapy isn't magic. I get that a therapist can't "do" something to "fix me"—but I always left feeling like it was a waste of time.

"So, tell me what happened when you were fourteen, when your eating disorder began. Did you ever encounter any abuse? Tell me more about the relationship with your parents."

JEEEZZZZZUUUSSSS!!

This was exactly how every session with every new therapist started.

Who cares!? I would think. *I am not fourteen. I am not four. I am right here, right now, with this problem. What can we do about it?*

I have always been action oriented and repeatedly going back to when I was fourteen, dissecting the beginning signs of my anxiety, felt so pointless. I gave it a real shot though. I engaged and showed up and put the effort in. I tried a few therapists over the years because I know that not everyone is a match, but every time, I left feeling like I had just wasted an hour of my life.

After the failed therapy attempts, I sought out a local psychologist who worked with eating disorders. I was convinced this was the guy that was going to help me! I didn't need to talk about anything; I needed medication to make me stop eating!

I had decided the only way for me to stop eating like a high school quarterback was some kind of medication. I googled several before the appointment with him so I could help expedite the process. I didn't want him saying he wasn't sure of what any were. I was coming prepared! I was desperate. At this point I was bingeing and purging five to ten times a day. I just wanted help to stop eating.

"You don't understand," I told the psychologist. "I feel like I have no control. I can't stop once I start. I am so tired of it. I just want to eat like a normal person. I am just so tired."

And he nodded, wrote some notes down, and scheduled a follow-up appointment after suggesting I see a dietitian. He said my weight wasn't high enough for an appetite suppressant.

What he didn't understand was that I didn't want the pill for weight loss! I wanted it to quiet the chaos I felt pulsing through my brain 24/7. I just wanted to stop thinking about food!

I felt like I was screaming down an empty hallway.

I was exhausted by thoughts of food, eating, burning off what I ate, thinking about what I would eat later, counting calories, all of it. And now I was exhausted by trying—and failing—to make myself understood.

I felt like my problem was never really taken seriously. When I would tell people, "I can't stop eating," or "I feel out of control around food," a frequent response would be, "Oh yeah, totally, me too. I am always SO hungry!"

Or "I know, girl, I have got to stop eating Sour Patch Kids." Or "Good thing you are so skinny! You should be happy!"

I found that people who haven't lived with an eating disorder don't really "get it." They can try. They can read and educate themselves. They can support you and be a great friend . . . but there is always a bit of a disconnect.

I felt defeated.

I felt hopeless.

But at the same damn time, I wasn't sure I was ready to let go of bingeing and purging. I wasn't sure how you could hate AND love something so much, but I did.

It was how I filled my day. It was what I did when I was bored or lonely. Normal people may call a friend or go for a walk or even go out for ice cream. I went to four fast-food drive-throughs, parked in a deserted lot, and ate until I couldn't taste it anymore.

Food made it so I didn't need anyone else.

FOOD ISN'T JUST FOOD

"I just want to be able to eat a bowl of cereal, Mom," I said through tears.

We were driving to Portland, heading toward what would be my first round of eating disorder treatment. At that point, my mom finally began to understand, a little bit, the constant hell I was in with food. She later told me, "When you said you couldn't eat a bowl of cereal—it broke my heart. I didn't realize how much it was consuming your life."

To most people, cereal is just cereal, right? Who cares? It is delicious any time of day!

Not for me. Food was *never* just food. It was carbs, sugar, calories, exercise, fat, weight gain, fun, excitement, punishment, guilt. Every bite, every meal, every calorie was taken into great consideration.

And it was *nonstop*.

I never just *casually* ate something. In fact, when I saw people do this, my brain broke.

I would see brides on TV shows going to a bakery and trying several bites of cake to decide what they wanted for their wedding day and wonder how they did this. Did they restrict all day for those few bites? Or maybe they, too, were throwing up? Because when I looked at how thin and beautiful they were, I knew there was no way they just ate bites of cake like that without preparing for it or planning how to burn it off somehow.

I simply could not wrap my brain around it.

Part of me felt jealous, part of me felt baffled, and part of me felt superior. I prided myself on the knowledge and willpower I had around food—but at the same time, I wanted nothing more than to just not care. I so desperately wanted to be the person who went out and got pizza with friends and laughed and was lighthearted. I wondered what it was like to not be so stressed out at events that the only way you could relax was to leave and eat a bunch of food until you couldn't feel.

It started out so harmless: just wanting to drop a few pounds. Tone and tighten, you know? And it worked; when the compliments came in, I actually did feel better for a minute. But then, before you know it, you're measuring your peanut butter, weighing your oatmeal, fishing out the yolk from your egg, and convincing yourself you really do love the protein-enriched, low-carb ice cream that tastes like asshole.

Going to treatment was something I agreed to—eventually. It wasn't my idea. My mom was strongly pushing me to go and I was tired. I was so tired. Tired of obsessing and counting and running and tracking and never knowing how to turn it all off unless I was asleep. The compliments on my body had slowed, and the women who used to gawk over my ability to not eat had flipped their awe to quiet concern only voiced to my mom. "Is she okay? She looks really thin. What are you going to do?"

So I agreed to go.

And I was also terrified. I was terrified because I was walking into my biggest fear—gaining weight.

I felt like a turkey the month before Thanksgiving. I knew that by going into treatment I was willingly asking to be fattened up. I knew one of my goals would be weight gain, and here I was, walking into the fire. But I wanted it. I so desperately wanted peace in my mind. I wanted the freedom I saw in others.

Well, for the most part . . .

There was still a large part of me that did not want to let go of the control I had over food, my body, and my weight. A couple of weeks before entering treatment, I started restricting severely, trying to get my weight down even lower, which I knew was unproductive. I mean, I was willingly going to treatment for help, and here I was pushing myself back even further.

But that was kind of my song and dance. Always fighting myself. Every day I woke up I felt like I went into battle with myself.

And this, my friend, is the worst war you can ever be in because everywhere you go, there you are.

CHAPTER 3:
JUST A DASH OF VODKA

If you have any problem in life you think can't get much worse, just add alcohol.

It wasn't a "first sip and I was hooked" kind of thing. The first time I got drunk, it was on Corona at a New Year's Eve party. I was fourteen, and my sneaking tendencies were already developing into a solid skill set, as none of the adults had any idea I had snuck a few beers into my room. It didn't take much for me to start feeling the effects. A little looser, more lighthearted, and a lot more laughter. *If a little is good, a lot must be great!* I threw back another one and it was all a great time until the next morning when I am pretty sure I uttered the ever so famous "I am NEVER drinking again!" statement while running to the bathroom to throw up, hoping my parents didn't hear me.

My stint in eating disorder treatment was tolerable at best. However, it wasn't long after my discharge that I spiraled back into my old habits. It wasn't entirely against my will, yet there was a part of me that felt compelled to revert. I believed I was an exception to their rules. The diet they prescribed seemed absurdly inappropriate for someone like me. What might have worked for others was simply not suited for ME. The excessive carbs were unnecessary; my body craved more greens and significantly more physical exertion—they just couldn't grasp the unique needs of my physiology.

I obsessively searched for the bread with the fewest carbs, scrutinized every detail on nutrition labels, and began following fitness influencers relentlessly. I sent online trainers photos of my current body and my "goal body" desperate for their secrets and routines to help me sculpt a physique that matched the ideal I envisioned in my dreams. Now, complicating my quest further, I introduced alcohol into the mix, adding another layer to my ongoing struggle to shape my body and my life on my own terms.

After my time in treatment, regaining some weight, and feeling slightly more in control of things, I wanted to get back to "normal," to regular life things, so I did what you are supposed to do . . . I attempted college.

I had hated school up until this point, and I was excited at the idea that college would finally be different. And it was just the next obvious step in life. I was eighteen and everyone knows that after high school you go to college if you want to have a happy and successful life. I saw the timeline in all the movies, I was fed this idea by countless teachers, peers, and parents—and I wanted it. I wanted my own "happily ever after." I was tired of being the one with all the problems, and I just wanted to be normal.

I was so ready to be out on my own! I wanted freedom, I wanted to find my friend group, I wanted to start moving on with my life! But . . . I was an absolute mess. Still.

A familiar pattern emerged at college: I woke up and went to the gym before eating could interfere, because my workouts, maintaining control, and burning calories were still my number one priority. I skipped about fifty percent of my classes. I knew where every single Grocery Outlet or cheap restaurant was within a five mile radius. I knew where all the garbage cans were to dump my bags of trash after a binge. I also knew where every single bathroom was and the cleanliness of it, because purging in filthy, smelly public toilets with dirty water and a smell so bad you wanted to die was not my go-to if I could help it.

Everything I wanted was slipping through my fingers, and I was doing it to myself. I could see it happening, but it was like an out-of-body experience. I was watching myself set fire to the life I wanted.

I made friends—eh, maybe a better way to say that is I found out their names and said hi a few times—with some of the girls on my floor. I wanted to connect, I wanted tons of cute photos plastered on my door or mirror of all the memories that were being created and would last a lifetime—but most of the time, I just ended up isolating myself to eat or exercise.

It was this split personality. I wanted to hang out and eat popcorn and watch movies. I wanted to effortlessly eat pizza and laugh about what had happened that day during class—I wanted it so badly. But I couldn't. I got so anxious it felt like my skin was going to melt off. My brain would start racing: *What do I say? Do they like me? What does she eat? I wonder if she has an eating disorder? I don't think they like me. I never fit in. What is wrong with me!?*

I couldn't take it. Within the first hour into any event or outing, I'd say I was tired, had somewhere else to go or somewhere to be, and then I'd retreat to what I was comfortable with: McDonalds, a tray of cupcakes, or absurd amounts of chocolate. And then I'd wonder why I was so lonely and had no friends. But the truth is, I didn't have space in my life for real friends *and* binge eating. I had to choose, and the food kept winning.

I realized I never had the practice of just "hanging out." In high school, I was never able to build that skill. It was completely foreign to me. I didn't know how to go to a friend's place and chat and watch TV. I didn't know how to enjoy a dinner with others and hang out afterward. I'd never done it! So when I was in a *normal* situation that *normal* people do, like having a group study night, going out for Thai food, or watching a movie, it was like asking me to juggle knives while doing somersaults.

After a few months in college, I had the lay of the land mastered in the same way that I did at home. I knew all the loudest doors and the best bathrooms and paid attention to everyone else's schedule so I would know when I could get my binges in.

I was back to living a double life—always on the lookout, always on edge, always a ticking time bomb. I wanted everyone to leave me the hell alone and let me eat and live the way I wanted. But I also desperately wanted a hug, to feel accepted, and to be a part of a friend group.

One great thing about being in college though, was that underage drinking was completely acceptable. The chatter, the running around, the always-on-the-go energy I learned could be quickly and quietly soothed by vodka. I played around with alcohol some during high school but not much because I was in my anorexic/

regimented phase so all those extra calories were an easy no. And I couldn't be staying up late drinking when I knew I had a workout to get in first thing.

Alcohol quieted my mind in the same way food did, but better. Alcohol allowed me to relax, to sit, to be with myself—but there was one benefit provided that food couldn't offer: it made me not want to eat.

Cha-ching!

The answer to my problems!!

Another secret to the universe I had finally discovered. Another secret that would finally allow me to stay skinny, manage my food, and do all the life things you are supposed to do.

Or so I thought . . .

You see, there's a slight difference in impact between bingeing on bagels and bingeing on booze and that is—being drunk. When you're binge eating, sure, you may be uncomfortably full, you may be distracted, but you can still show up and no one can tell. You can drive around, you can have conversations, you can go to work. Being drunk is a little more difficult to sneak under the radar, as I'd discover.

There was no denying I was doing a horrible job taking care of myself in the dorms at college. I would frequently call my mom hysterical. Sobbing about not being able to stop bingeing and purging. Sobbing about not having friends. Sobbing about clothes fitting different or not having any money (bulimia is a VERY expensive habit). My grades were plummeting, which wasn't surprising because I pretty much never went to class. I would start off strong. I had all the textbooks, notebooks, and colored pens. But after a few weeks, I would be in the middle of a binge I couldn't stop or so full I couldn't move and skip. And after you skip once, it's a quick and slippery slope to never going back to class again.

After less than a year of living in the dorms, I moved off-campus to live with my brother. It felt like a sigh of relief; being near my brother was like a weighted blanket of calm. Even if things were chaotic, I felt okay. I lived with him and three of his friends and it was great!

This is the change you needed! This is what's going to help you stay on track.

I had my own room, I was living with great people, and I felt like it was all going to be fine.

It lasted less than nine months.

Turns out, changing your environment does not change you.

If my relationship to food was a slow burn, my relationship to drinking was a wildfire.

It took over my life. What started as having some Mike's Hard Lemonade Light (because duh) quickly morphed to purchasing hard alcohol so I didn't have to deal with so many bottles to dispose of.

I have few regrets or moments of absolute disappointment in myself in my life, but the ones I can remember all involve alcohol.

Like the night Randy got a call: "Hey, um, I think your sister is here. She is curled up on our floor. Drunk. And she peed her pants."

He arrived at the house party I had crashed, peeled me off the floor, and put me in his car with frustration pulsing through his pores. Once we got home, I had to do the walk of shame through our house in front of about seven people with piss-soaked pants.

I'd wake up the next morning with some pangs of regret, put on my running clothes, and decide this day was going to be different.

I thought food and binge eating turned me into a monster, but alcohol turned me into a monster *and* it directly impacted other people. I started stealing alcohol from other people in the house. I tried to make friends based on the age of the person. Under twenty-one, no thanks; over twenty-one and I would carefully and meticulously widdle my way into your life. I had a constant rotation of people of legal age who could buy me alcohol. It was a curated system that allowed me to not burn out one source too quickly or let this one realize, "Yo, this chick is crazy AND an alcoholic!"

I kept the charm on for as long as it took for me to get another half gallon of Potter's vodka—the largest amount of alcohol I could buy at the cheapest rate. I may have been bad at school, but I was great at working out ways to keep my habits alive and thriving. I was resourceful and I was manipulative.

After more failing grades, no longer being able to flirt my way into getting alcohol purchased, a breakup with my only boyfriend ever, and completely destroying the college dream I'd set out to create. I threw in the towel. I called my mom sobbing again, and I knew she felt for me. I could hear the heartbreak in her voice. She wanted nothing more than for me to just have a normal, happy life too. I decided to move back home.

School was another thing I failed. *What is it going to take? What is wrong with me? Do I need a brain transplant? Do I need to be locked in a prison cell and have food passed through to me with no way to get out and get more?*

I couldn't not binge. I couldn't not purge. I couldn't not drink. Unfortunately, some things have to get worse before they can get better.

YOU PROBABLY KNOW AN ALCOHOLIC

I'm not sure, but I think my mom may have thought part of my increased drinking was due to being away at college, the stress of that and just being in a more stressful, party-like atmosphere. Maybe she, too, because I honestly did, thought being back home would help me relax and get back on track with life. That it would give me a minute to catch my breath, get a job, find myself—and all those things you're supposed to do when you're twenty.

I, however, did none of them.

I didn't get a job. I didn't socialize. I didn't do anything.

My drinking went from a gin and tonic at 8:00 p.m. a night, or two a week, to three gin and tonics. To then having a drink at 4:00 p.m. while lying by the pool, to something at 11:00 a.m. because why not?

My mom started to notice this wasn't just an occasional drink I was having. This was becoming a daily routine for me.

The slack and understanding she had for me initially was wearing thin.

"Renae, it is 11:00 a.m. and you are drinking."

I'd brush it off, distract her with something else, or tell her the handful of things I had done around the house until she let it go.

But after several weeks of her coming home to find her daughter passed out by the pool after she put in a full day of work, she had had it.

"You are getting a job. Get your ass up. Get dressed. And go get a job or you aren't staying here."

The patience and understanding she had for me when I initially moved back in had evaporated. She should win an award for how long she lasted though because I was a sloppy, rude, inconsiderate kind of drunk. The kind that thinks she is cooking up a masterpiece in the kitchen, but, in reality, everything is inedible and the kitchen looks like it was run by toddlers and puppies.

Burners would be left on. Food was on everything. A sink full of dishes. And I saw no problem with any of it.

I did what she wanted. I got a job at Starbucks. And you know what? I loved it. I loved working the morning shift; I enjoyed the wave of customers we got and a bar lined with coffee cups waiting to be made. I loved the pace and tunnel vision I could have while I was there. I enjoyed getting to work with people and have relationships with customers.

My dad was also proud of me. He would frequently come in and see me, order a coffee, get some beans, and chat for a few. He would say it was a great job for me and how I could grow with the company if I wanted!

Things were working out. I was making money. Holding down a job. I even got invited to do things with coworkers a couple of times.

And yet . . . When I would come home, the house would be dark, I had nothing to do and wasn't ready to go to sleep . . . I'd think, *I can have just one.*

I had a couple of good months where my drinking was manageable. I was showering regularly, going to work, making friends, cleaning up after myself. I was really doing it.

And it was like it all flipped within about forty-eight hours.

My nightly drinking escalated quickly. It reached the point that when my 3:45 a.m. alarm went off to get ready for the opening shift at work, I would wake up still drunk but also hungover. I would run to the bathroom and dry heave into the toilet, watching my green mucus colored bile climb down the toilet bowl, leaving a chilling and repulsive taste in my mouth. I was beyond thirsty, but I was unable to keep anything down for more than a minute or so. The first three hours at work were excruciating. I had to come up with excuses for why I was going to the bathroom so much, but the pain in my stomach and body was so strong, the only way it was relieved was to try and throw up or be crouched down. There was nothing in my stomach, so I tried muffling the retching sounds of my dry heaving and coughing with frequent flushes. My mornings of running in and out of the bathroom were getting harder to mask. I used as many excuses as I could—I was emptying the trash, mopping the bathroom floor, changing the toilet paper, saying I started my period.

"Renae, we couldn't find you. Where were you? We need you on bar."

"Oh, I was just cleaning the bathroom. Be right there!"

And despite always being in the bathroom, it was never actually clean, which I am sure was one more strike my manager had against me. Things only got worse. The awful feelings lingered longer and became unbearable. And that was when I stumbled upon the dangerous realization that drinking more could ease my hangover symptoms.

I will just have a little in the morning to even me out so I can function and keep my job.

I did that for a little while, but the buzz and balancing out I had at 4:00 a.m. would start to wear off after a few hours, and the shakes, sweats, and nausea would come back. I had to get creative. I started going to the gas station on my lunch break and getting fruity flavored beers, or whatever option they had that I thought the smell would be most easy to mask, and pounding them down one by one in my car, shoving the cans under my seat before clocking back in.

I was making it work.

I had a routine down.

Wake up, shot of vodka, work, six pack at lunch, try to leave work early, go home and pass out, wake up, drink, try to make it through the evening without my mom noticing I was drunk, drink, go to bed, repeat.

But then my manager called me into the office one morning. It was her and one other supervisor. "Renae, we don't mind what you do on the weekends or when you aren't at work, but you can't come into work smelling like alcohol."

CUE PLAYING DUMB.

"Oh, haha, weird. I must have spilled some on my sweater the other night."

They weren't buying it.

"We think you need help. You cannot keep working here."

And that was the first time I was fired due to my drinking—but not the last!

You probably know an alcoholic. That's what I've come to discover: if you aren't one, you are about two degrees of separation from one. If you work in the corporate world, you may know some functioning alcoholics. The ones who believe "it's five o'clock somewhere" at a noon lunch meeting. The ones who you have no idea how they made it into work that morning when you saw them the night before and they were in bad shape. The ones that occasionally reek of booze and you wonder what else might be in their morning coffee. But they showed up. They clocked in.

They made it out after work for drinks. They kept up appearances.

My window of being that kind of alcoholic was short. I would say it was almost nonexistent.

I didn't really "drink." I slammed hard alcohol, or whatever I could find, until I couldn't stand up.

I never got dressed up and went out to bars and sipped on fancy cocktails over dinner. I have never had a glass of wine with a meal. I have never enjoyed a mimosa with brunch. I went from zero to one hundred. There was NO middle ground.

I know what you might be thinking: "Why didn't your parents just throw away your alcohol? Why didn't your mom just forbid you to drink? Why didn't they stop you?"

Here's the thing about most of the addicts/alcoholics/anyone with any sort of addiction that I know: you are one resourceful and manipulative son of a bitch. I had bottles of alcohol hidden everywhere. I mean *everywhere*. Under sinks, in shoes, carefully placed outside around the perimeter of our house, in the orchard, nestled inside bushes. I knew the odds of someone finding one bottle was pretty good, but nine? Never.

When I was drunk, I didn't care about anything, because I didn't think. My only focus was to get fucked up. That was it. I didn't care who I hurt or what it took to attain oblivion. I was uncontrollable. Unruly. Unhinged.

And slowly, but surely, this led me to more insolation. My way of drinking was repelling the people that I would normally drink with. You know you're not doing good when the people in your drinking group think you have a drinking problem.

I was unemployed and my only goal in life was drinking more.

It's hard for me to even describe and convey the way I was going about life. To fully explain the lack of regard I had for anyone or anything. I cared about no one and nothing except myself.

I stole money from my parents, I was destructive, I was mean.

The drinking got so bad that I would have moments, maybe an hour a day, where I would be in this weird in between phase. Not drunk enough to not care but miles away from sober. And everything I was doing came crashing down. It was like a window I could see my own life through and I hated it. During one of those windows, my mom was able to get me in the car and drove me to a detox center.

Of all the things I have ever been through in my life, going through withdrawals was the most terrifying. Upon arrival at the detox center, I was visibly intoxicated. They checked me in, went through all my items thoroughly, and took my shaver and some of my toiletries that had alcohol in them, then I fell into my bed.

A day or two later, while I was sleeping, I saw a rat. I sat up in bed. "Am I dreaming?"

As I sat there, I started seeing more rats. I stood up on the bed. "What is happening?"

Hundreds of rats were now flooding the floor, and they were coming toward me. They made their way onto the bed and me. I screamed. I knew I needed out of that room. How would I get out though? I jumped on the rats, ripped the door open, and ran out hysterically.

"RATS!!! There are RATS!!!"

I was sobbing.

I ran into the common area, which had a few other men who were there to detox too. Rough looking guys.

"Rats?" said the employee on duty. "Are you sure? Maybe a mouse but not a rat." He went in to check.

I was shaking. Snot was coming out of my nose. As I was sitting on the couch, rocking myself back and fourth, I noticed a tiny spider on my arm. As I looked at my arm, it started getting bigger, more started to appear, they were now swarming both of my arms and jumping on to my face.

"Please someone please help me! PLEASE!" I screamed again, pleading with the men around me to do something.

Despite the state I was in, I recall looking at the man next to me; I can't remember much about him other than his beard and leathery skin. I heard him say to someone else, "She is experiencing withdrawals."

Then he turned to me, put his hand on my back, and said, his voice empathetic, "You are okay. What you are seeing isn't real."

And I realized he was right because for brief moments the spiders would be gone. And that made me cry even more.

I was taken to the hospital because that facility was not suited for someone in my condition. I was just as chaotic and anxious in the hospital waiting room. I kept seeing things that weren't there, I kept hoping the spider would not come back, and I was getting more vocal. Finally, after a little more yelling and crying, someone came into the room, and the last thing I remember was getting a shot in the ass and then it was lights out.

REHAB, ROUND I

I was twenty-one, *finally* able to legally buy alcohol, and there I was checking into rehab.

Driving up to the facility, which actually looked more like a small apartment complex, I noticed several women standing outside. I got out of the car with my duffle bag, and there were no warm welcomes, no smiles, no kind greetings. The women on the porch didn't break from sipping their coffee and smoking their cigarettes with the exception of obviously sizing me up and down. My country club going, Nordstrom shopping, privileged, anorexic ass stuck out like a sore thumb.

I ended up living here for the next three months, and it was absolute hell.

After a few weeks, when the alcohol was completely out of my system and I'd oriented myself, my eating disorder returned in full force. It was like she was just lying dormant, biding her time while I was boozing it up, but the second the booze took a back seat, my eating disorder was limbered up, ready to take the stage.

My counselor got wind that I was stealing food and throwing up. She called me into her office one day, gave me a toilet bowl cleaner, and said, "Here. Take this. And think about this every time before you throw up. And if you throw up, you have to use this to clean the toilet. You have to walk in front of everyone while carrying this so they know you threw up too."

I was mortified. Ultimately though, this made me more angry and determined to binge and purge to spite her. It felt like me against the world.

I didn't *want* to binge and purge, I didn't *want* to drink. I wanted to be normal! I wanted to have friends and eat soft pretzels at the mall, and to have a boyfriend who I wanted to spend time with. I wanted to be able to relax and watch a movie. I wanted to be able to go out for a spur-of-the-moment ice cream. *I wanted to feel safe and at ease.* But I couldn't, and it felt like no one understood that.

I knew what I was doing was wrong, but I couldn't stop. It would be like telling someone to stop breathing.

My food, my body stuff, my binge eating and purging—it all came YEARS before my drinking. But no one seemed to care about that. No one seemed to understand that if my food wasn't the issue, my drinking probably wouldn't be either!

I eventually graduated from that hellhole of a treatment center, and I had never been happier. Yes, being sober was nice, but I really wanted outta that place! I transitioned to living in a clean and sober house, and even though I was still a mess in the eating department, so much confidence and energy came with being sober.

I started feeling whole again.

TOO GOOD TO BE TRUE

Getting sober turned me back into a functioning human again. It took several months, but I was finally feeling good again. I had ambitions and goals and wanted to do something with my life! I no longer wanted to lie around doing nothing. My energy returned, my sense of humor came back, and I was ready to get the ball rollin' again.

I got a job at a local eye doctor's office and felt so proud of myself for the first time in a long time.

Finally! I am not the problem child. I get to be a normal person!

I was five months sober. Legally employed. Getting regular paychecks. I was back in society! I was really doing it! I was ready! I was so ready! This is it! "I am never going back to that other life."

I was back to running again which weirdly was one of the few times I craved a drink. Any time I went for a run on a hot day, I would crave a beer after—or some kind of alcoholic beverage. Probably because I was still bingeing and purging which dehydrates the hell out of you, and followed up with running, doubled down on the dehydration. Aside from that, no drinking thoughts were that prevalent.

After rehab, I moved into a sort of "transitional house" that was owned by the rehab I had just left. There were a handful of other sober women there, and part of the deal with living there was that you agreed to random drug tests and you had to have a job. "No problem!"

On a particularly good day as I was driving home from work, I decided, *I'll go to that little Italian place. I'm going to treat myself to a nice dinner for one.* It was this little spot I had been eyeing for a couple of months. I passed it each day to and from work.

I walked in with my scrubs and I felt extra confident. Like, "Look at me, I am obviously a functioning human because I have a job that requires you to wear scrubs. So you know I am going places in life." It wasn't a very nice Italian place, plus it was in a redneck town, so wearing scrubs wasn't weird.

I sat down and looked at the menu.

The server came to the table.

And "I'll have a gin and tonic, please" fell right out of my mouth.

I hadn't preplanned this, but after I ordered it, I really thought, *I am pretty sure I can drink now.*

I ordered two more and decided to only get a salad for dinner so as not to soak up all the booze and kill my buzz.

On the way home, I stopped and got a six pack.

Within a month, my drinking got so bad I lost my job as the eye doctor's receptionist. I didn't call, I didn't text, I just stopped going—apparently that is grounds for firing—who knew!

The great news (maybe that isn't the right word for this particular situation, the ironic news?) was that a week or so before drinking at the Italian restaurant, I had decided I was ready to move out of that sober house and started looking for a different place to live.

The day they gave me a urinalysis at my house, which I would inevitably fail and be kicked out, my dad told me he found another sober person to live with me. *Meant to be!* I thought. The sober person was a guy in his late twenties.

I got hammered the day I moved in. Which was me drinking half a fifth of vodka and passing out on my unmade bed with boxes and bags surrounding me. The next morning, I woke up and found my sober roommate passed out with a fifth of whiskey next to him.

We lived together for less than two months. Apparently I was walking around the house naked, and he and his friends stole my laptop while I was drunk. My dad could clearly see that this was not the situation he had hoped for. I didn't have money for rent as I was unemployed again, so I talked my dad into letting me move in with him. I had tried to move back in with my mom, but she was beyond done. She had been dealing with my bullshit for long enough; she said, "It's time for your dad to step in."

CHAPTER 4:
HAVE YOU SEEN RENAE?

Things started off okay, as they usually did right after I made a move. I got a job at one of the nicest restaurants in Walla Walla, Washington, as a hostess, and I was thrilled. I loved the restaurant scene and the people who were attracted to the restaurant scene. I loved the intensity, I loved the buzz of being slammed and seeing a line snaking out the door. I loved the way everyone worked together like a finely oiled machine to keep tables turning and money coming in.

Maybe I can manage this place. Maybe I should go to school to be a restaurant manager. I was always thinking ahead. Always thinking about how I was going to be successful one day. I wasn't sober, but I wasn't out of control. Sure, my drinking over the last couple of months had picked up, and most mornings I woke up puking bile and shaking before I had a couple of shots to calm my nerves, but I was maintaining. I was able to show up to work, get my job done, then go to the afterparty with the kitchen staff and managers. I knew if I could just hang on for those five or so hours at work, I could start drinking steadily.

This was how I operated: never completely sober, trying not to get too drunk, and planning my every move around booze.

I was pretty good at moderating myself during my shifts. I would get a nice buzz on before the shift actually started, usually taking my last couple swigs in my car in the parking lot; it just made the night go better. But then it would wear off. I would be dragging halfway through my shift because I started sobering up, and it took everything in me not to curl up and go to sleep. So I began putting vodka in a water bottle and keeping it in my purse. At first I was terrified to take it in, certain someone would find it, but after a few shifts, the fear wore off and I thought it was my best plan.

I would make several trips to the back to "check my phone," where I would carefully take a couple sips and follow it with several pieces of gum to mask the odor. Then, the rest of the night would be a breeze! I was more fun, more lighthearted, more flirty, and everyone else seemed better too.

The vodka would land in my empty stomach, and I would feel as if I had been shot up with adrenaline. I lived for that part. One night though, the careful routine I had created hit a roadblock. I had a little too much.

I was doing my normal work routine: greeting guests, taking them to their table, answering calls. I was making my normal trips to the coat closet and eating all the gum. Things were going all right as far as I knew.

"Welcome in. Two?"

A couple had arrived and I was walking them to a nice table in a back corner of the restaurant and then . . .

I have no clue.

The lights went out for me after that. I have no idea what I did, what I said, or what happened, and to this day I am too scared to ask. I recall getting in my car with eyes full of tears, thankfully, making it to my dad's house safely.

The next day, I was called in to "talk." I was in the chef's office, talking about the night before, and the skill of lying and manipulating that I had honed to keep all my addictions alive came out in full force.

"You were drunk, Renae. You were clearly drinking on the job."

"No, I wasn't."

I had crafted a plan that morning to try and keep my job.

"I was drinking but not at work. I had this mixed drink at a friend's house, and I guess I didn't realize how strong it was. I also take antidepressants." I had brought the bottle with me and put it on his desk for proof. "I think whatever was in that mixed drink created a reaction."

My body felt like a thousand pounds. I felt hollow inside. I felt tight. I felt worthless. Alcohol was usually a portal into the carefree, lighthearted way I wanted to live, but right now it had led me down a path I didn't like. I was ashamed of my behavior. Mainly because I had no clue what happened. I had no idea what I did after taking that couple to their table. And at that meeting I was sober. I could feel the pain of embarrassment and disappointment, and it was gut-wrenching. I tried coming up with excuses for my behavior, and I begged to get my job back, but they weren't having me.

My drinking was taking on a life of its own. The option to drink or not drink in the evenings was diminishing, and it was becoming more of a must. The anxiety would become so palpable, the nights would feel so long, my thoughts would be so loud. The only way to get through was a drink—or seven.

Since moving into my dad's place, he also quickly realized my drinking had been taken to a new level. He tried setting rules that there was no alcohol to be brought into the home or consumed in the home. He would often have a beer with dinner but switched to water or lemonade to offer extra support. I continued sneaking airplane size bottles in my pant pockets or secret compartments of my bag. My dad enjoyed making beer as a hobby and kept all ingredients and end products, and we lived in the Walla Walla Valley, so the wine was always plentiful. He quickly learned this was not going to work though. After a few nice requests and orders of **NO DRINKING**, which I brushed off without hesitation, the fridge was now wrapped several times in chicken wire to keep me out. In addition to that, he set an alarm system at night to keep me from escaping. He frequently searched my room for alcohol and took my house key so I could only come and go when he was there. He did everything he could to keep me alive without making me a prisoner.

However, it was all about to come to a head.

When I was deeply intoxicated, I became convinced that I was on the brink of a seizure and death. So I'd call 911. By this time, I was a frequent flier at the local hospital, and the nurses had seen enough of me to know my drill. I'd probably been in three times in the last month, and they were over it. This time, I was there for a few hours—long enough to be coherent, but far from sober. They sent me home before I was fully stabilized; I'm sure they did this because they were simply exhausted by my antics, which included full panic attacks, repeatedly asking if I was dying, requesting fluids, peeing myself, and just being downright rude. Since I got there by ambulance, I didn't have a ride home. My dad was out of town for the day, and, honestly, I just wanted to avoid that whole interaction anyway. So the hospital provided me with a ride from one of their house cab drivers. The driver arrived, I got in, and he took me home. We chatted a bit, but I can't remember what we discussed. My head was empty, my body felt weak, and I just needed a couple drinks and to lie down. When we got to my dad's place, he wasn't home; the doors were locked, and all the windows were sealed shut.

Shit! Now what?

"Everything okay?" the driver asked.

"Oh, my dad won't be home until tonight and everything is locked. I can't get in."

"You can stay at my house," he said. "No one is home." Even in my state, I knew that was kind of strange. Who was this man in his fifties, inviting twenty-one-year-old me to his home? But when you're drinking, when you're drunk, the normal instinct to keep yourself safe is dulled—or, for me, nonexistent. I felt invincible but also didn't think about much other than the next three seconds. I am not sure, but I think he told me I could drink at his house, and that's what sealed the deal for me. Once I was in his living room, I was finishing my first beer and cracking the second.

I wish I could remember everything that happened that afternoon, but I don't. I sloshed in and out of consciousness. Hours passed and I opened my eyes at one point, still in the living room on the couch, and saw a teenager across the room, visibly disgusted by me. The man had mentioned his ex-wife would be stopping by. I don't know why he was telling me; I could barely hold my own head up. But I do remember her coming in, looking at me, absolutely disgusted by the sight of me. I overheard her say, "What the hell are you doing? She needs to leave!"

I went back to sleep.

When I woke up, I was back home at my dad's house. I have zero recollection of how this happened. My dad later informed me he discovered I had gone to the hospital and that I had last been seen getting medical transport home through the hospital taxi service. They managed to get an idea of where the cab driver lived from the hospital and drove to that part of town. While driving around, Ellen, my dad's wife, saw someone sitting outside and asked if she had seen a red head with an older man from the hospital. And she said yes, and pointed to the house across the street. Ellen then went from normal female strength to superwoman and bolted into that home, picked me up off the couch, and carried me out the front door to my dad's car before my dad even knew what was going on.

As I started rustling around in my room and waking up more, my dad and his wife heard me and told me I was staying in that room upstairs where they could keep tabs on me until I detoxed. They locked the door and carried on with their evening. Moments later, I was grabbing one of my dad's sweaters and putting on a pair of his slippers. *I am going to get something to drink.*

As sneakily and quietly as a very intoxicated person could manage, I unlocked the window and pushed out the screen. It was probably a twenty-foot jump, but when you're drunk, you don't feel pain.

I may not have felt it, but the adults certainly heard it. THUD! I hit the ground and started running.

The problem with this plan—there were many problems—was that I had no ID. I had no money. It was the middle of the night. I was wasted. But worst of all, my dad was living in a Seventh-day Adventist community, and they didn't even sell alcohol in the area. AND all the stores closed at sundown. I didn't think about any of that while I was jumping out the window.

It didn't take long before I heard, "NORM! SHE'S GONE!" My dad's wife had discovered I was on the loose. I knew I didn't have much time. I spotted a house with its lights on one street over and ran up to the door. A woman answered, and before she could even see my face and with no pretensions at politeness, I said, "Hi, do you have any alcohol I can have? Anything at all?"

Yes. That is exactly what I said. And you may be shocked to hear her response, because I know I was. She didn't invite me in for a cold one. "Honey, call the cops!" she yelled to her husband.

My dad and his wife were shouting for me, so I took my cue to leave. I bolted off her porch and crawled under a parked car. I'm still not quite sure what my goal was here, other than don't get caught. Of course, I did. The jig was up and I slid out from under the car. My dad grabbed my arm, and we walked back to the house. I was pretty unfazed by the whole situation. Had I been sober, that would have been a debilitatingly shameful event. However, had I been sober, that never would have happened. Booze had such a great way of evaporating all emotion. Which is one reason I never wanted to get sober. Who wants to deal with the regret of last night's decisions?

When we got home, they sat me on the couch and decided to let me sip on one beer to keep me from going into withdrawals. Eventually, I went to bed.

It was a day or two later that my dad approached me. "Sweetie. I found another rehab. It isn't too far. I think you should go again."

I did NOT want to go back to treatment. "Dad. I can get better! I just had a bad few weeks. I am getting better. I can do this." But we both knew there was no way I could do this. We both knew I was an alcoholic, and as much as everyone wanted me to be able to stop drinking or drink normally, I couldn't. And then we both started sobbing. Have you ever seen your parent cry? It is the worst. Knife in the chest, absolute worst.

I agreed to go back to treatment and try it again.

DING DING DING, ROUND 2!

Six months after my first treatment center, I was packing my bags for round two. This facility felt like a dream compared to the first one. My room, still shared, was larger and gave me some of my own space. The meals were cooked for us instead of us taking turns cooking for everyone, and there were a few spots to walk around outside or just sit outside. I felt much more comfortable here than I did at the first place, but despite it being nicer, cleaner, and more organized, I received similar "support" around my food issues.

I don't know why exactly—perhaps it's because I told my counselor I struggled with an eating disorder—but it was only about a week before I caught on that someone was shadowing me and taking note of everything I did. If I went to a vending machine, someone wrote it down. Anytime I went to the bathroom, someone noted it in my file. Anytime I left a group, I was followed. I had a session with a counselor who said, "We know what you're doing. We are onto you and you need to stop."

I was blindsided. Didn't they know I hate this more than they do? It was like they thought I had a choice or loved what I was doing. Like throwing up five times a day was my idea of a good time. Or secretly eating three packages of Pop-Tarts, some Red Vines, and chocolate was my ideal way to decompress and move through life. It felt like my entire treatment team was against me, and I was pretty sure that's not how treatment is supposed to feel.

I was being transparent, asking for help with my food issues and discussing my anxiety, but all people wanted to do was talk about my childhood and my drinking.

But while I was there, I met a lady who "got me." She said she'd gone through her own food issues and suggested I do what she does each day: eat a peanut butter and jelly sandwich at lunch then immediately go for a walk.

So I did. I sat down, I ate a peanut butter and jelly sandwich, thinking about the sugar in the jelly, the carbs in the white bread, and that fat in the peanut butter, and then we walked. We jogged. We ran. I believe we were running from similar demons.

The company was nice, the distraction was helpful, but it was all temporary. The calmness I felt in my mind, the distraction from my body, was all just a placeholder.

I continued to wonder if the only way I would be able to stop bingeing was if I went to prison and food was slid to me through a mail slot. And really . . . Would that have even been so bad? I mean, portioned food, ample time to work out, no way I could binge, and I could stay thin and gain muscle.

Hey! Maybe I'm onto something. Maybe prison was what I needed!

Thankfully, I never went to jail, nor did I join the Navy, which I seriously considered and even went as far as taking the ASVAB (Armed Services Vocational Aptitude Battery) test. I thought maybe if I went into the Navy, I'd stop drinking, be forced to work out all the time, have beautifully structured days, and they'd whip me into shape. The Navy would strengthen my willpower, and I'd come back as a changed woman. (I was informed later that the Navy is a horrible place to go if you're wanting to cut back on drinking.)

Despite feeling defeated and misunderstood by my treatment team's failure to understand my challenges, and my food issues being completely tossed to the side, the booze thing needed to be resolved first, which I couldn't see at the time. I thought and knew my food was the reason I had reached for alcohol to begin with, and by addressing the alcohol, I felt like they were completely dismissing my biggest issue. In hindsight, I realized that if you aren't coherent, able to shower and take care of yourself, it will be impossible to do anything else. I was physically addicted to alcohol at that point, I needed to be somewhere safe, and I needed to be monitored. My family and friends were proud of me for getting sober (AGAIN). I'm sure many were holding their breath, not wanting to say too much, not wanting to get too excited, fearing the moment when the other shoe would drop, but also just glad I wasn't destroying everything in my path and drinking to oblivion.

I gained a little weight since I was finally consuming solid food, and I started looking a little less like an emaciated alcoholic and a little more like a functioning member of society. I showered, put on makeup, and got dressed. To the untrained eye, I was a functioning human. I was "better." And for a while, I felt better. But I knew if I didn't figure out this food thing, my sobriety would only be temporary.

I wish I could say this was the last time I drank.

CHAPTER 5:
GETTING SOBER

Over the next year and a half, I was fired from several more jobs. I stole alcohol from grocery stores, I was kicked out of every place I tried living in, and I dined and dashed from most restaurants on Eighty-Second Avenue in Portland. I got into cars with people I didn't know if they were buying alcohol, I went into apartments with strangers if they said they were partying, I blacked out in public places. My inhibitions, fears, and instinct for self-preservation could not withstand the copious amounts of alcohol I was consuming.

This is something I've heard from a lot of people with addictions, and although I try to stay away from cheesy clichés it's true: I cannot believe I am still alive.

I cannot believe I was not raped. I cannot believe I did not kill someone while driving drunk. I cannot believe I was not arrested. When I think back to how reckless I was, I feel sick. When I think back to how ruthless, destructive, and hurtful to others I was, my chest gets tight and I just want to shrink down to nothing.

When I reflect on the hell I put my family through and what it must have felt like to see their daughter wasting away, eyes rolled back in my head, completely out of control, never really sure if I was alive or dead—it's almost unbearable.

But here's one great thing about being a fuckup early on in life: the bar you set is low. Like trying to limbo under a pole glued to the ground low. There literally wasn't anywhere else to go but up.

I needed to experiment a little more after that rehab. I needed to be certain I couldn't drink responsibly, because you know what? I wanted to! I desperately wanted to be a normal drinker. I didn't want to be sober. I didn't want to go to meetings. I didn't want to have another problem. I wanted to be normal.

The few times I tried drinking after rehab, I went down fast. I could drink like a "normal" person for a day, maybe two, but before I knew it, I was on my way to the liquor store for the biggest and cheapest bottle of booze I could find and dying to get home so I could drink until I passed out. I'd had a taste of sobriety. I had enough time sober in that rehab to see that the old me was still in there. My joy was still in me. My ability to exist without consuming alcohol was possible.

"I don't think I can drink."

This was a very VERY hard statement for me to wrap my brain around, as I am someone who wants zero limits or restrictions on anything. The second there is a "You can't do this," I am doing it. But I had exhausted every effort to drink in a controlled way. I had lost damn near everything and everyone. I turned into something I despised when I was drinking. I didn't care about anything other than more alcohol. I started to recognize that my personality, my genes, my whatever is inside me and alcohol, they don't mix. You know the volcano you made back in grade school with baking soda and vinegar, and you watched it erupt? That is what happens to me when you add alcohol.

I was finally coming to terms with it.

And now we're back to the very beginning of this story, to the day my mom finally lost every ounce of patience and compassion for me and hurled my bag of belongings into what would be my new home.

"YOU NEVER DRINK?"

Getting sober as a twenty-two-year-old sucks—or so I thought at the time. *This is supposed to be my prime! What am I going to do at my wedding for the toast? Will I have to have a "dry" wedding? Oh my god, no one will come to a dry wedding, that is so stupid. My life is over.*

This is what we call overthinking and future tripping. You may be familiar with the process. I had JUST peeled myself off the floor I'd passed out on and stopped pissing my pants on a nightly basis, but I was very concerned about my wedding, despite being extremely single.

I was twenty-two! I was supposed to be getting dressed up and going out on the town, drinking fun cocktails and dancing the night away. But instead, I was in a room full of strangers who were all forty years older than me, who I really did not want to be associated with. I felt robbed. The years I'd heard so many wonderful things about were being swallowed by AA meetings and buttoned down in a clean and sober house. This was not what I had in mind.

But even though it wasn't exactly what I'd wished for as a little girl, none of it was as bad as living another year in a blackout.

The first couple of years were rough, which I now know to be true for most things. Life never really happens on the timeline we had planned. When I went out to social events with people who weren't sober, I was terrified they'd notice. I rehearsed what I'd say if they asked why I didn't drink. I felt like such a freak. Not drinking, and telling people I didn't drink, felt like a huge deal to me. I couldn't imagine anyone wanting to socialize with me if they found out I was sober.

But you know what? No one cared. Some people would ask why. Some would give me a hard time and tell me how bad they felt for me. But no one really pressed me. Okay, sure, occasionally there was that one asshole who just would not let up, but that person was likely the alcoholic of the group. For the most part though, no one paid much attention. And the longer I was sober, the more I heard things like, "Good for you. I should probably stop too."

Without alcohol to take the edge off or escape into, I had to figure out who this new Renae was and what she did without drinking or spending time with other people who drank to get drunk.

What did she do on Friday nights? Or after work? For fun? How did sober Renae get through life?

NO ONE KNEW

My identity for most of my life was "the healthy one." The girl who had salad and carrots for lunch. The coworker who never ate the donuts in the break room. I heard comments like, "If we could just eat like Renae!" Or "If we could just work out like Renae." Women would ask me if I could help them lose weight. They wanted to know if I had exercises I could suggest to them and tips for willpower and motivation around food. I would just kind of laugh and shrug it off, all the while thinking, "If you only knew."

If you only knew the anxiety, panic, and self-loathing I carried around. If you only knew what I did when night fell. If you only knew how much money and time I spent eating food alone while scrolling through my phone and watching TV. If you only knew that when you asked me what I did with my food, I was dying to know what you did with yours.

But they didn't know because I never gave them any reason to. I worked, I worked out, I had friends, I had a car, I ate when we went out to eat, I did all the "normal things."

I had mastered it.

In fact, I would say I was an expert-level manipulator and bulimic. Don't they say after ten thousand hours of doing something, you become an expert? Give me the cap, gown, and diploma because I'm sure I had far surpassed that.

I didn't know who I was without my eating disorder to be honest. It felt to me like breathing does to you. You wake up and breathe. It's just a part of you. And I believed that all the chaos I felt around food was part of me. I couldn't escape.

I kept this secret of mine hidden from most of my work friends because there is nothing worse than telling someone stuff about your food and then feeling them watch every single thing you eat or feeling their eyes on you every single time you go to the bathroom. It's. The. Worst.

But some of my closer friends were aware. I openly disclosed it to them, hoping maybe they could do or say something that would fix me. But I often got responses along the lines of, "Just don't buy them. Can you stop when you're full? What if you have a strict mealtime? Maybe you should see a therapist." They were doing what they could to comfort me, but for people who don't stop at three fast-food restaurants on the way home and eat until they can't breathe or worry about the amount of calories in the milk the barista added to their coffee, there was a disconnect.

But, god, how badly I wished those suggestions worked. I'd tried so many therapists and meal plans. I had not bought the food, I had prepped all the food, I had cut out foods, I had had complete allowance around food, I had salted food to stop eating. I kept photos of women's bodies I desperately wanted to look like in my phone, I had personal trainers, I bought my own equipment to exercise at home. I lived with roommates and had no roommates, I got night shift jobs and day shift jobs, I got into relationships and stayed single. I went to OA meetings, FA meetings, and hired nutritionists.

The list went on and on.

But, despite my relationship to food and my body consuming my life, I still worked, I enjoyed weekend getaways, bike rides, dinner with friends, and dating. There was usually a little bit of an ulterior motive with those activities though, because I was typically planning them around helping me not binge (even though the friends didn't know that) or helping me burn off calories.

To an observer, I seemed "normal." I didn't look like anything was wrong. I laughed, joked, and did normal things. But I was so used to my food issues and my performance around them by then that it really wasn't that bad. It was just a part of my lifestyle. I knew to leave parties a little early so I could go home and eat the way I wanted without staying up too late. I knew the excuses to use and all the restaurants I could stop at on the way home.

Thinking back now, I cannot believe the time and energy I dedicated to eating, exercising, and trying to maintain my body. I cannot believe how much attention and focus it took. But, I did it. Because that's what we do.

We always get it done, no matter how much pain we are in. We push through.

CHAPTER 6:
BACK TO TREATMENT

With a few years of sobriety under my belt, I started feeling pretty good. I was studying nursing pre-reqs at a community college, doing VERY poorly I might add, but I was doing it. I was on track to become a nurse, and it filled me with hope.

"So what do you do?" people would ask.

"I'm going into nursing."

That was all I needed to say and people immediately followed up with "Wow! That is such a great job! Good for you. You're going to be an excellent nurse! There's a lot of security in that job!" I had a plan, and it was a respectable plan at that.

I eventually got a job at a major hospital, and I was on top of the world. I was finally doing something!

For years I had waffled with career goals. My resume was about three pages long—getting fired every three months didn't help, but I usually left those ones off and fudged the dates a little to fill in the gaps.

But this job felt real. Good pay, great benefits, and a set schedule. Whoa.

I was single at the time, smack dab in the middle of my twenties, and it felt like I was becoming an adult and finally doing life right. Of course, I was still way off the ten-year plan I'd written during my junior year of high school, which would have had me married, working in an office, with one kid and another on the way.

But I was doing it.

Me.

I—the family pariah, the one who always had ALL the problems and whose parents only ever heard, "How is Renae doing?"—was hopefully no longer going to be the highlight of conversation. I was going to have a normal, successful, happy life.

Except for one thing . . . I hated it.

I had worked so hard and studied so hard to get here! How could this be happening? How could I be miserable? How was that possible? Was there something wrong with me? Was I incapable of being happy and satisfied in life?

I had been working in the medical field for almost six years, and I really did enjoy it for a little bit, in the beginning, I think. I mean, it was all so great on paper. Each year, each new unit I worked on, each new certification I received, I made more money and gained more seniority. Every time I told someone what I was doing, their eyes lit up a little. "Wow! That's so great! Good for you! What a great job to get into. So stable and so rewarding."

Their excitement slammed into me like a brick, which is actually something I hoped for every day on the way to work. I started to hate my work so much I dreamed of getting in a car accident on the way in so I wouldn't have to go.

My shift was three days on and four days off, but the entire day before work, I spent it in gut-wrenching anxiety, which made it feel like four days on. I would dread the long day, the fluorescent lights, call bells, showers, hustling, being the lowest rung on the ladder, my lunch time being dictated to me, and having to wear a walkie-talkie so I could be reached at any second of my shift. It was claustrophobic. It was exhausting. It was stressful. And I hated it.

I created rules for myself around food. Since I wasn't able to just eat like a normal person, I established certain boundaries for myself to try and keep me from going completely off the hinges. One of them was "No bingeing at work."

I vowed I wouldn't do it. I knew the kind of person it turned me into; I knew I lost all focus once I started. I wanted work to be a safe space. A place where I hadn't identified where all the best bathrooms for throwing up were. Where all the garbage cans to throw my wrappers away were. Or the patterns and routines of coworkers so I could plan sneaking off and eating a bunch of food when I new they were occupied. But slowly, day by day, it started to return.

It was a slippery slope, one that once I started going down it, there were no brakes.

Soon after, I started purging at work, which, as always, spun me out to a new degree of being unhinged.

As well as showing up and doing my job, which was hard enough, I now had to manage an eating disorder.

The hospital kept the patients' area stocked with graham crackers, Tillamook cheese squares, fruit, and peanut butter, which I stuffed my pockets with.

I assumed the intensity I felt around "needing it" was similar to that of drugs. I'd binge to give me a boost of energy because by hour nine at work I was dead. I had nothing left to give. And eating gave me some adrenaline. Then, even though I'd just worked twelve or more hours at the hospital, I went home and started my second job, which was binge eating. It never stopped.

Chaos at work in the day and chaos at home until midnight.

The panic was building. I felt like something was going to snap. The thought of keeping up everything I was doing sent me into a spiral. I was at the end of my rope and something had to give.

A DIFFERENT FLAVOR OF HARD

Some people think hard is getting up at 4:00 a.m. when you are tired. Some people think hard is pushing yourself to the brink of exhaustion. Some people think hard is taking on way more than you can handle.

Hard for people like me and possibly you, is doing less. Hard for people like us is asking for help and admitting, "Actually, I am not okay."

And I was not okay. I had been living alone for the first time in my life, and it was as bad as I feared it might be. I was okay for a few weeks, but, slowly, I started bingeing and then purging and then I never left the house or opened the blinds unless I was going to work or to get more food. I was exhausted. I was spending so much money on food. My throat was constantly sore, face and eyes swollen from bingeing and purging for hours on end, and I just couldn't do it anymore. When I lived with other people, it at least forced me to stop, but when I was living alone, there was no reason to. Except for now I wanted to. The lack of socialization and constant eating was pushing my mood to an all-time low.

"So why didn't you just stop?" I couldn't. I felt like I had zero power. I felt controlled by something else. Every single morning, I would wake up and think, hope, and pray it would be different. I would plan out the afternoon and evening, yet every single night I found myself with an extra large bowl, a family size box of Lucky Charms, and double stuff Oreos, curled up on the couch with the TV going while also mindlessly scrolling through my phone. There was so much stimulation going on and yet my brain was completely shut off. It was like the only way I could get a break was having chaos all around me. I finally asked for help.

Even though my dad had JUST helped me move into this one-bedroom apartment, I had to tell him I needed help moving out. Because despite wanting to feel independent, wanting to have my own space and life, I was proving to myself I couldn't. It wasn't just the eating that was bad, it was that I feared I would start drinking. I feared the only way I could stop eating was to drink, and I was terrified of that. I felt as if my options were keep eating and ultimately turn to alcohol. Or slowly kill myself with my relationship to food. I decided to go back into treatment for my eating disorder, and this time it was a different type of hard.

I carried a lot of pride in how strong, confident, and independent I was. I was seen as a leader, someone who got things done. To admit I couldn't do this alone, that my food was feeling so out of control I had to completely exit my life and go live somewhere out in the forest for months was . . . embarrassing. Mortifying, actually.

Are people going to think I'm faking it? Are they going to think I just want a vacation? What about the women I run with—what will they think? What about that coworker I never talk to but I think she's really awesome, what is she going to think? What do I tell people? Do I lie? How is this still a thing? Why can't I just get it together? What the hell is wrong with me??

Do you know what they said at work? "Go. Please. Take care of yourself. It's okay. Come back when you're ready."

Part of me wanted to indulge the thought that they hated having me work there. That me leaving for a few months was the world's best gift to them and they'd talk about how screwed up I was and that they'd been waiting for a break from me since I started. But I didn't. I had to choose to believe they really did care—that they understood, they enjoyed working with me, and they wanted me to get the support I needed.

Driving to treatment, I spun in a maelstrom of emotions. Part of me felt a huge sigh of relief: the nightmare was ending. But, like every other time I had gone to treatment, another part of me was terrified.

I had no idea what was in store for me over the next several months or even how long I would live there or what it looked like. I arrived late because I needed to get one last binge in, one final hoorah! Because at that point, I only knew two ways to exist around food, which was either super clean restrictive eating or bingeing. The idea of being able to feel anxiety without a bag of Reese's Peanut Butter Cups felt impossible. To eat a few and not the whole bag seemed surreal. Even though I hated my relationship to food and I hated the bingeing, there was something so comforting about it. The familiarity of it. The momentary silence I felt in my brain.

For the first couple weeks, I was exhausted. I couldn't stay awake. Anytime I was on the couch for more than twenty minutes, my eyes started to burn and I had to sleep. The constant exercising, bingeing, purging, and obsessing had been exhausting, and I was finally able to relax. And I could do so without food. Which was just further proof to me that so much of my "go go go" attitude was the tornado of binge eating and feeling terrified to be with myself. I'd been doing that for years and I finally felt safe. My food was portioned and served to me. I didn't have a stash of M&M's in my room calling me to eat them even if I didn't want to. I didn't have to worry about who was coming and going or when I could eat or when I should work out. I could just relax. My brain could relax.

Nights were different. For the first couple of weeks, once or twice a night, I woke up shivering in a lake of sweat. The sheets were so wet and cold I had to lay bath towels down and sleep on them until I could change the bedding in the morning. The nurse told me it was completely normal and that it was my metabolism kicking in.

My metabolism? Really? It felt so . . . extreme. Like something the girls with anorexia might experience, or someone with a real problem would go through—but not me. Not someone who was living life, had a job, exercised, had some social circles, paid bills, and such. But the sweat streaming out of my body told a different story. And with the increased metabolism came increased hunger.

Feeling ravenous or stuffed was excruciating for me. For years, either of those feelings meant something bad was coming. Hunger signified a binge on its way; fullness warned of a purge (or a binge) on the horizon, and I did that dance for years. I didn't know how to just be with it. I had no idea how to be hungry or full and be okay.

I could feel my hunger intensify. I pushed through the hunger pains for a while because honestly, I would have loved to have been in treatment and on a meal plan that made me lose weight. I didn't want to acknowledge that I felt so hungry most days I was distracted by it. I kept thinking the feeling would go away, but it didn't. I got so hungry I noticed myself trying to figure out how I could binge, which was when I got honest with myself. I didn't come here to keep doing what I'd always done with food. I came here to do something different.

During a movie one night, I pulled a staff member aside. "Hey, um, I'm really hungry. I can't even focus on the movie because I keep thinking about eating. If I were released today, I would go find as much food as I could and eat it as fast as I could. I think I need a snack."

She looked at me suspiciously. "Hmm. Have you talked to your dietitian about this?"

I suppose she had to ask me. I'm sure women in all different places with all different intentions came into eating disorder treatment and would lie and manipulate the same way I saw drug addicts do in addiction treatment, but it was offensive to me at that moment. She was questioning my request to eat. My hunger. I was finally listening to my body, and someone was raising their eyebrow at it. I was told I could have an apple and sat down at the dining room table alone to eat my extra snack.

Eventually the dietitian increased my food and my hunger balanced out. I wasn't the bottomless black pit of consumption I thought I was. Eventually I stopped sweating at night. Eventually I started feeling "normal."

It was like a hundred-pound boulder I had been carrying around that I was finally able to set down and rest on. I wasn't thinking about food. I filled out what I wanted to eat, someone cooked it for me, and that was that! The other ninety-five percent of my head space was finally free of food noise. When I got tired at 8:00 or 9:00 p.m., you know what I did? I went to sleep. I didn't force myself to stay awake to finish off the last of whatever I was inhaling that I could no longer taste just so I could finish it; I just went to sleep. After meals, I felt satisfied. True satisfaction. I was full but I wasn't so full I was in pain. I was full in the sense that after the meal, thinking about what I had eaten or what meal was coming next was nowhere to be found. I was able to watch TV without simultaneously inhaling a bag of chips. I had the ability to sit and focus and learn how to knit. I was able to read a book! Sitting still before felt like my skin was melting off, and now I was getting cozy in a chair with a blanket and reading for an hour. WHO AM I?!

So, this is how normal people live! This is so easy! I thought.

I was finally out of fight or flight. I was finally safe. I was no longer running from myself. The mental ticker in my mind going a million miles an hour wondering where I'd get my next binge foods, what bathroom I would throw up in, how I would get my workout in, or what everyone's schedules were so I knew the windows of time I had to eat and then clean up the evidence, were all gone.

Going into treatment was one of the hardest things I'd ever done, but treatment itself was a breeze for me. Everything was portioned and doled out; I didn't have to think. I never had big emotions I couldn't handle while I was there, and my body didn't change much. When I got bored at night, eating wasn't an option, so I didn't. There was no "real life" stuff to stress over, so emotional eating wasn't an issue. I wasn't "underweight" when I went in, so I wasn't put on a restorative meal plan or required to gain a certain amount of weight. Everything was like clockwork: meals were set, snacks were set, outings were set. Some of the other clients and a few of the staff were annoying, but nothing I couldn't handle.

After three months of residential treatment, I was ready to get outta there and move the hell on with my life!

One of the friends I made during my stay there (we're still friends today) said, "Renae. You have a tendency to think you're ready before you actually are." That statement stuck with me, and you know what? She was right. That trait, which some may see as a character defect has, I think, kept me going. That drive burning deep down within me has never let me give up. So, yeah, it may mean I jump before I can see the next step, but it has also kept me alive. It has given me an edge to keep pursuing what I really want for myself.

My friend was right, but I honestly felt I had gotten everything from the treatment center that I needed. I hadn't binged or purged in months. I was able to concentrate and read books again. I could sit still and relax. I could eat bread without bingeing. I'd started incorporating exercise again. I was ready. And eventually discharged.

TRADER JOE'S

I was supposed to go back to work at the hospital after my leave of absence for treatment, and they agreed to work around all my outpatient support appointments. But the thought of returning to that job brought all the anxiety I'd left behind flooding back.

I can't do it. I can't go back there. I can't stand the long shifts and the work. I do not want to do it.

I hadn't anticipated feeling that way, but after three months of no longer using food to numb and escape my life, I'd stepped into a new level of clarity and also trust in myself. My body was telling me NO. The pay was good, the benefits were great, the work was fine, and the thought of it made me want to crawl into a black hole and die. I can't even explain why; I just knew nursing, the field I wanted for so long to be a part of and which I'd spent years pursuing, was no longer it for me.

I had no idea what I was going to do, but I knew I couldn't go back there. One day, I bumped into an acquaintance, I had dated a friend of hers at one point, updated her on what I had been up to and how I was looking for a new job.

"Come apply at Trader Joe's. I will put in a good word for you."

So I did! And got the job!

From the first day I stepped inside for my interview, it was a full-body YES from me. *Who are these weirdos?* I thought while filling out the paperwork, watching the staff come and go out of the back room. There was laughter, there was joking around, there were some four letter words, there was work being done, and there was a laid-back energy.

I knew this was the place for me.

On my first lunch break, eating among coworkers in the break room, I noticed something.

No one was talking about their diet. No one was commenting, "Oh, I shouldn't be eating these free cookies that were left out!" They just shut up and ate the damn cookies while scrolling on their phone, or didn't eat them, and it was no big deal. Their lunches were also actual lunches. Breads, burritos, noodles, sandwiches—substantial meals. And I then fully realized how disordered the break room was in the hospital. I always hated eating there and was never sure why; now, it was clear.

At the hospital, no one ever shut up about their diet. Someone brought bagels in once and a nurse said, "I don't need that because I don't want a bagel here," and pointed at her midsection. It was impossible to eat anything without everyone commenting on it or talking about their new eating plan. Turns out, health professionals are also messed up around food, and hospitals are an extremely fatphobic environment. Who knew? But none of that noise was occurring here. No weight loss challenges, no posters on the walls telling you to eat this, not that. Just people eating, working, and looking at their phones. What a relief.

For the first time in all the nine hundred jobs I'd had, I felt like I could actually be me. For the first time, I thought, *I belong here*. That might sound a bit melodramatic—I mean, it's a freaking grocery store— but what it taught me was when you fit in somewhere, *you know*, and when you don't, *YOU KNOW*. Shoot, several of the staff didn't even like me and I *still* felt like I fit in! That's how good this place was to me. I have always been a hard worker and I have always been energetic and weird, and wouldn't you know, Trader Joe's loves that shit!

I finally felt like I was stepping into my own path.

INDULGENCE

For about six months after leaving treatment, I ate what and when I wanted. Partially because I was terrified of restricting and going back to the binge-purge cycles I had freshly clawed my way out of, but also because it was fun! Did you know you can just order whatever the hell you want whenever the hell you want as an adult? I feel like this perk isn't talked about enough! It wasn't like before when I was hiding it. I was ordering meals and eating ice cream in a calm way for all to see. If I wanted cake on a Tuesday night, I went and got some. I was eating cereal every morning, kind of as a "fuck you" to diet culture and my past life which NEVER allowed me to eat cereal, but also because it was really freaking good. I was enjoying a bowl of ice cream each night as a before-bed snack, a part of treatment I carried through after leaving. The satisfaction and sheer pride I felt in myself with being able to dish myself up a bowl of ice cream, eat it, and then go to sleep was a little overkill, but, listen, when you used to polish off pint(s) alone in your bed at midnight, shoving the container to the bottom of the garbage can hoping no one finds it, this kind of living was something to be excited about.

The thought of vegetables made me feel nauseated. Which was a harsh shift from my previous life of my meals being ninety-five percent vegetable to get the sensation of being full without the calories. But I couldn't stomach it. Salad as an entrée? Are you kidding me? Gimme the turkey club and soup! I wanted comfort food. I felt a little out of control, but it was NOTHING compared to the binge episodes I'd had in the past, and I was grateful for that. Being out of treatment and eating more decadent food, and just more food in general, my body began to change. I felt fairly normal around food, yes, especially because all I had to compare it to was the shit show I was existing in before; however, eating cake multiple times a week, ice cream nightly, eating handfuls of chips because "fuck you (diet culture, Instagram models, weight loss programs, the world!), I can!" was starting to change my body. A change I soon found out I was not prepared to handle.

I now realize there were several major points that weren't addressed in treatment, such as:

- Our culture's deeply embedded fatphobia
- Body acceptance (not love, not like, just acceptance)
- The fact that our bodies are constantly changing
- Legalization of food—the phase of allowing foods, which is also typically a time you want more carbs/sugar/previously restricted items
- Managing emotions without eating

I guess it's possible they did cover these things and I missed it because I wasn't ready to hear it, but I honestly don't recall learning about any of this.

What I was going through was some legalization. When you've been restricting yourself for years and you finally stop, it's common to go through a period where you want all those foods you never had permission to freely eat. For many people, that's carby or sugary items. I was unaware of this though. I had no idea this was a thing until years later. It was all fine and dandy the first few months, but as the indulgent eating continued, some of the panic set in while my body started getting a little softer, bumpier, and bigger. Pants got snugger. I was sure my arms had tripled in size. My face felt huge.

I can't keep doing this! If I keep eating like this, I will never stop gaining weight! I can't believe how irresponsible I have been to let my body get to this point!

And this moment of panic is when most people resort to a diet, which I understand because, as you'll see, I did it too.

DRESS SHOPPING

My brother and his partner were finally getting married! I'd been out of treatment for about a year, and I was working, living life, and overall doing all right. My relationship to food wasn't perfect, but it was pretty good considering. The icing on the cake: I was asked to be a part of my brother's wedding which meant I got to do all the bridesmaids activities. Since my friendship group was pretty nonexistent for most of my life, this was the first wedding I'd ever been in.

As we all arrived at David's Bridal to try on dresses, I felt more self-conscious in my body than normal. I knew the other girls in the wedding party, but I hadn't seen them in several years and couldn't help but notice how thin they were.

My internal monologue was on form as we walked into the store. *How are they so thin? How am I no longer the skinniest one? Have they always been this way? No, Renae. It's okay. It's fine. You're fine. It's not a big deal. You're taking care of yourself. You just got out of treatment. It's okay.*

We found a few dresses and went to the fitting room. The store didn't have a huge selection of sizes on the floor. They kept a few on hand for you to get an idea of what it looked like, and if you wanted it, they could order it. We picked two or three we all liked, then realized we'd all have to try that one dress on due to the lack of sizes. So, each girl would try on the dress, come out and show the rest of us how it looked, then go back in and slip it off so the next person could have a go.

When it was finally my turn, I bounced into the fitting room, excited to see how it fit on me too. Except, it didn't fit. I couldn't zip it up. *How can this be!* I thought.

My heart sank, my body felt so heavy, and I wanted to disappear into the floor.

I was the only one in the group who couldn't fit into the dress. My sister-in-law, being the absolute best human that she is, did her best to make it no big deal (because really, in hindsight, it was no big deal). I desperately wanted it to be no big deal too, because this was her day, not mine.

But it was such a big deal to me. By the second or third dress I couldn't effortlessly fit into like everyone else, I could barely contain the tears that were threatening to flood my cheeks. I took deep breaths and tried not to lose it. I fake-laughed and made a monumental effort to not let on that the ground had been ripped out from beneath me.

I was mortified, disappointed, and embarrassed. How could I let this happen to myself? As soon as I left the store, the tears streamed down my face. I decided, *That's it. I am going to get healthy! I am going to lose weight.*

OLD HABITS DIE HARD

If there is one thing I am good at, it's pushing through discomfort.

I feel like a "skill," for lack of a better word, picked up through addiction and disordered eating is that these things give you one hell of a pain threshold. You learn how to completely detach from your body. You learn to shut off physical cues of pain, hunger, and exhaustion. You push through, no matter what.

I was mortified in that fitting room and at that wedding in my body. It felt like a foreign object to me. I felt the urge to tell people ahead of time, "I know I look bigger now than before, and, well, I just want you to know that I know, and I am working on it."

Today, when I see pictures of myself from that time, my heart aches for me. My heart aches for the way I talked to myself and treated myself because I looked great. I was a normal and acceptable weight. I just looked like an average person. Like, you could tell I ate dessert and wanted bread to be wrapping my sandwich and not a bell pepper, but it wouldn't surprise you to know that I also worked out sometimes. At the time, I felt like such a disappointment. Like I was letting everyone down. Who exactly? Who was everyone? I wasn't even sure, but I just knew people were disappointed and disgusted by me. I was itching to get out of my own skin.

When you feel threatened or scared, you go back to what feels familiar. You don't think about the consequences; you don't care—your only focus is safety. Unfortunately, my brain was still confused about what was safe and what wasn't, and my eyes still distorted what looked okay and what didn't.

I pushed people away and focused on my workouts again. I concentrated less on what I wanted and only on what I knew was the right thing today. Goddamn it, wouldn't you know, it worked. I guess that depends on what "working" means to you, but for me that looked like dropping weight quickly and getting into what I would consider to be the best shape of my life. I was in an almost manic state for weeks. I couldn't sleep, my body felt like it needed to move constantly. My food was solely vegetables and protein. And I refamiliarized myself with the comfort of hunger. I remembered how easy it was to push through the pain. I remembered how strong I was. However, like always, it was temporary. And just like before, the compliments flooded in. As I religiously worked out and tracked every morsel I consumed, people showered me in praise: "Wow. You look great! What are you eating? What's your workout routine? Can you help me lose weight? How do you have so much willpower? Will you teach me?"

And you know what? I didn't hate it!

In fact, the compliments and the attention made me feel . . . special. It felt like I had an edge on other people. I had started to discover something I was good at.

Since I was working out so much, the next step was obviously to do a triathlon. This may not be obvious to a regular person, but to someone with an "if a little is good, a lot must be GREAT!" way of approaching most things in life, it made perfect sense! It was a great way to push my physical limits even more. It gave me something to focus on and dig into. Sure, I had never actually done any swimming other than playing in a pool and tanning, but I loved the thrill of the idea of doing something hard. I was game. I was ready.

While I was excited about this new adventure, I kept it to myself for the most part. People recognized my body changing, weight dropping, and muscles poppin' and would ask what I was training for.

"Oh nothing. Just life." I couldn't tell them because . . . what if I bombed it?! If I had to drop out or drowned during the swim—I didn't want a single person to know. I would keep all the disappointment to myself.

I was in it. I was in the training. I was in the mentality. I was following triathletes on Instagram, I was getting books, I was learning about different types of bikes and gear. I was hooked. And hungry.

I was working out so much I actually couldn't sleep. So I would often get up at 3:00 or 4:00 a.m. and go for a run. I was ravenous all the time and eighty-five percent of my food was green. And damn, it felt good. During that time I had absolute tunnel vision. I was focused on my goal. I was eating paleo like a pro; however my gas was absolutely deadly. I was rippin' farts 24/7. So many times at work I'd let one off and run—hoping it wouldn't follow me. But I didn't care. I loved eating lighter, I loved feeling leaner in my body, and I wasn't going to stop. I looked in the mirror and loved what I saw. I mean, I *loved* it. I felt so strong. I felt so proud of my hard work. I felt so dedicated to my workouts.

The time was getting closer to the event. I had found a few groups to swim with and loved the community I was creating. *This is where I belong*, I thought.

I told my dad about the triathlon and the training; I knew he would understand the thrill of it. He and his wife decided to come up and support me on race day, which was great because it turned out I was actually pretty nervous the morning of. The whole time I was waiting to start, walking around looking for the place to put my bike, getting a number tattooed on my arm and calf with a Sharpie, squinting in the beaming bright lights while it was still pitch black out, I looked around in disbelief. *I can't believe I'm doing this.* Fifty percent scared shitless, Fifty percent high on caffeine.

Then I shut down the fear, taking some deep breaths, and worked to stay as calm as possible as I got ready at the starting line.

IT. WAS. AMAZING.

I felt great the entire time, and as I crossed the finish line, my friend skidded up and said, "You just placed second in your age group!"

"WHAT! Are you kidding me?! How? How is that possible? I don't know what I'm doing!" I didn't have a triathlon bike, I didn't have cycling shoes, I didn't have a fancy triathlon outfit or one of those douchey-looking aerodynamic helmets that men are always wearing when riding their bikes around town and that always look a BIT overkill for a Tuesday roll through the park. And I just placed second. Hot damn.

I received a constant state of congrats from friends, family, and people I barely knew. I was riding high.

For a couple of days.

My mom came up a few days after to celebrate with me, because heaven forbid she and my dad be present at the same event, but my mood had started to change. Was it just because I was around my mom? Despite loving her more than life itself, she had a special way of getting under my skin. We were sitting in the living room, and I had a breakdown. "Mom, I don't know what to do. My binge eating is back, and I've started throwing up again, and I don't know what to do!"

There's something about being around my mom that brings out all the softness. My tough exterior faded away. I could be an absolute sobbing mess; I knew she wouldn't judge me. I knew she wouldn't be angry. I knew she would make me feel better.

"Oh, Renae. You were doing so well! What happened? Was it training for the triathlon?" I was crying, she was holding me. "You know I don't care at all about you doing triathlons or how well you do at them. I just wanted to support you. Don't ever do another one again, and that will be fine by me."

I could see the pain she was feeling because of the pain I was feeling. Which made me cry even harder.

I *had* been doing good. For a couple of months leading up to the event, everything had been PERFECT! Everything was so dialed in and going according to plan.

Or so I thought.

Rebounding from an extreme often looks like doing the opposite in equal intensity. All my clean eating, high energy, and rigorous training was followed with extreme lows, feeling wildly out of control around food, and hating my body even more.

My high from getting second place was quickly swallowed by the realization that I could never do another triathlon, because how on earth would I be able to beat what I had just done? What if I did a second one and got tenth place? What would people think?

Everything came pouring out of me as my mom hugged me. "Oh, sweetie, I would rather you get last place in a triathlon and enjoy it than go through this."

Last place was never an option for me. I did things to win. To be the best. To quiet the demons inside my brain. I didn't know how to live in the middle. I didn't know how to not use self-hatred to motivate myself or how to not compare myself to every other breathing soul.

I was so tired. Physically and mentally.

I was tired of the same cycles I had been living in for fifteen years. I was tired of bingeing on the same things over and over.

I was so tired of thinking, *After this, I won't do it again,* only to do it again. I was so tired of pushing myself and feeling like I had to be on.

I was so tired of fighting against myself.

But I really began to wonder if it was even possible for someone like me to live any other way.

CHAPTER 7:
"RENAE, MOM FELL"

The day it happened, I had been doing surprisingly well with my food.

After three colleges, twelve years, many starts and stops, several trips to rehab, a handful of degree changes, and all the ups and downs, I had reached my final year at Portland State University.

I knew social science was not going to be a lucrative choice for a degree, but I also knew that pretending I could go for something like engineering or bio-chem was a joke. I had heard from countless people, "It doesn't matter, just get your college degree." So that was exactly what I was doing.

The pressure of school sent my eating into complete oblivion. I would sneak bags of Red Vines,

M&Ms, granola bars, and sandwiches into my book bag so I could eat and study. It was actually a very unproductive way to focus, but it felt like the only way I could sit still. That day, however, my food was surprisingly good! I was dressed in real clothes, not workout clothes, I had eaten lunch like a normal human being, and I wasn't feeling manic, panic, or drained. I was pretty proud of myself! It was close to finals week, and I was in the school library doing research for a paper that was due soon.

Then, I felt my phone vibrating. It was a call from my brother.

There are about three people I always answer phone calls from; everyone else, just text me if it's that important.

So when I saw his name, I quickly and excitedly answered. "Hey, Rand!" I said in a hushed voice because I knew phones weren't allowed in the library computer area.

"Hey, Naes, how's it going?" I told him about getting ready for finals and being in the library. "Hey . . ." he said. "So, uh, I guess mom fell this morning . . . and it wasn't good."

"What do you mean?" I said, very confused by that sentence.

My mom, in her early sixties, was certainly not the epitome of health but by no means was sick, unstable, or fragile. She was tough. Stubborn. So "mom falling" really didn't compute in my brain. I kind of thought, *Okay, if she fell, she should just stand up.*

I'm not sure how much he actually knew at that point and if he was telling me everything or keeping things vague to help keep me calm.

"She's at the hospital in Walla Walla. And it isn't looking that good."

I heard what he was saying but it wasn't going into my brain. I'd just messaged her on Facebook that morning to tell her my boyfriend and I had gotten back together, again. We chatted briefly, and she said she had painting to do that day. This couldn't be that big of a deal, but why would she be at the hospital? Did she have a broken arm or something?

I grabbed my stuff, threw it in my backpack, got in my car, and headed toward eastern Oregon. I drove in silence. I drove fast. And I felt sick. So many questions were swirling through my brain, but I knew she would be fine. She was painting and fell, it's fine. But not being able to see her and assess the situation with my own eyes was killing me; I needed to be there.

After two hours driving, at around 6:00 p.m. as dusk fell, I got another call from my brother. "They're life-flighting her to Harborview in Seattle." My gut sank. My hands started shaking. *This cannot be happening. How is this happening? This cannot be happening. This doesn't happen.* I pulled over, turned in the opposite direction, and started toward Seattle. After the longest drive of my life, I arrived at Harborview Medical.

My brother, his wife, and my dad greeted me. I was shocked to see my dad there and wondered what my mom would think, but I was so relieved to see him.

"You can go see her if you'd like. She's on a breathing tube and is unresponsive."

I walked through the large doors of the ICU and saw my mom lying there hooked up to so many tubes and machines. I held her hand and kept waiting for a little squeeze from her. I knew she was going to be okay, and I just wanted a little squeeze. I pushed back the hair they didn't have to shave off and looked at her helplessly lying there.

"She's gonna be so pissed they shaved her head when she wakes up." We chuckled.

Hours passed, I think; I'm not sure. We had no update from the doctor, so minutes felt like days. We just waited. We paced in and out of her room. We drank coffee. We looked at our phones. And we waited.

She will be fine. She has to be, I kept saying to myself. *She will pull through, and she may have a long road ahead, but she will be okay. Next year at this time, we aren't going to believe this happened!*

My mom was always outspoken about how she never wanted to be hooked up to machines. "Just take me out and shoot me!" she'd say in her blunt and matter-of-fact way.

Finally the doors to our private little room opened. And the doctor said, "I am so sorry . . ." And I knew exactly what that meant.

It couldn't be true. I wanted to demand that he do something, that someone else come to assess her, but all I could do was scream into my wadded-up jacket and melt into the couch I was on. I really, truly thought she would be fine. I thought he would say, "She's awake now, you can go see her." But he didn't.

We spent the next several hours wrapping our heads around the reality of the situation. The situation that a fall, which was likely caused by either a stroke or brain embolism, was what had killed my mom.

We waited for my mom's sister and mom to arrive from Spokane so they could say goodbye. I went in and out of the large ICU doors, passing by the nurses station, feeling sadness all around me. I saw the hurt in the nurses eyes, I saw the tears streaming down their faces. I would stand by her bed, hold her hand, and think, *How?*

Shortly after my aunt and grandma arrived and said goodbye, we removed the breathing tube.

I was messaging with her on Facebook that morning, and now I was watching her take her last breath.

I left the hospital. I left my mom.

I looked the same, but I would never be the same.

AFTER MY MOM DIED

Have you ever lost someone close to you? It's such a strange experience. It seems fake at first. Your brain can't really comprehend that they're gone. And then the fragility of life is crammed down your throat.

You look around and see things in a completely new way. You realize how stupid everything you've been worrying about is, how much time you waste on things that don't matter. You see how lost you get in the silly details and how you forget the bigger picture. You're slapped with the reality of just how quickly life can pass, and you feel such a strong urge to get out and really live it. A lightning rod of "LET'S START LIVING" shoots up your ass and the things you've been shrugging off and settling with are now front and center.

In addition to this onslaught of new emotions and fresh perspectives, I was baffled. I didn't understand how I could be going through something so life-changing while no one really cared. "No one" being the rest of the world. People kept going to work. TV shows kept running. Friends kept posting on social media. It was surreal. My life stopped, but no one else's did. I felt like a character in a movie who had come back to life and was walking the streets, but no one else could see me. I was living on a different planet, mentally.

After she died, I felt like I was grieving wrong. This voice in my head constantly told me to be more sad or just do it differently somehow. I was out running one afternoon, and someone waved at me and I smiled and waved back, and then the gut punch came. *What are you doing, Renae? He's going to think you don't even care that your mom died a few weeks ago. You're not only out running but you're smiling and waving! What is wrong with you? You shouldn't have looked so happy!*

After we had the funeral, I started getting back to regular life—or I tried, at least . . . I was working at a nonprofit helping homeless vets. I was on the "right" track, at least according to society. I worked full time, I had regular hours, and I was helping people. I was in a field related to my degree and . . . I'll be damned if it didn't feel completely wrong. Again.

WHAT IS WRONG WITH ME! Am I incapable of being happy? Of just living a normal life? Words I'd said and thought many times before. *I hate this job. I hate this life. But I have no idea what I'm supposed to do!*

So I quit.

Again.

I quit another job that made sense. I quit another path that might have actually led me to something. Did I secretly not want to be happy and successful? Did I actually want to be miserable forever? Did I have such commitment issues that I would never be able to stay in a job, relationship, or do *anything* for more than two years?

It sure felt like it. But I couldn't ignore it. After my mom died, the importance and tenderness of life was hurled at me. My bingeing and food stuff wasn't awful at that point; I mean, I'd lived with it for so long it was basically just baked into who I was, or so I thought. But after she died, something shifted inside my brain. It wasn't overnight, it wasn't like an electric shock or burning bush moment; it was more like slowly peeling back the layers. I started thinking about myself and my life differently.

What am I doing? Like, what am I REALLY doing? I don't want this. I don't want this job. I do not want to spend another ten years bingeing and hating my body. I don't want this.

I'm not religious in the traditional sense, but I think part of the reason my mom died was for me to finally get out of the torment and torture I had been trapped under with food. She went through every treatment and every rehab with me. She paid for all my new clothes because I frequently called while having a meltdown in my closet. She listened while I vented on the phone about being lost; she poured all of herself into helping me be happy and have a good life. It was after she died that something changed inside me. I got serious about creating happiness in my life.

When my mom died, there were so many things she hadn't done. She told me how she wanted to be a veterinarian but her dad pushed her into dental hygiene. How she didn't want to live in the town where we had lived my entire life, but my dad kept her here. She had plans to retire and travel and finally live life the way SHE wanted, and she never made it.

I was both terrified of that happening to me and more inspired than I ever had been before.

Because you know what? My mom died with some debt. She died with friendships. She died with food in the refrigerator. She died with things in the mail still being sent. She died with trips planned. She died at a weight she didn't love. And guess what? None of it mattered. Seeing all that happen, it changed me.

I had spent over half my life and almost all my free time, money, and headspace worried about my body. Bingeing in isolation. Lying about being okay. Fearing weight gain. Counting calories. Killing myself with exercise. And on and on. For what? What had it gotten me? What had maintaining an "acceptable" body really done for me? What could I look back on and think, *Damn, I did that.* It was a hamster wheel in hell. Obsessing about food and losing weight feels productive, but in reality, it doesn't do shit. Even when I looked back on old photos of fun times, I was instantly hit with "Oh, I hated my body then." Or "That's when I was trying the Whole30." Or "I remember how bad my food was then."

Every event in my life up to that moment was overshadowed by how out of control around food I felt or how uncomfortable in my body I was. It followed me for as long as I could remember, and I was sick of it.

If I have to gain weight to regain my sanity and freedom, fine! I will do it. I don't care. I just want this cycle, madness, and obsession to end! I just want to feel normal around food. I just want to move through my day without always thinking about my weight!

And that, my friend, is a state of surrender. It is the most freeing and amazing moment of your life. It is when you decide to stop fighting yourself. It was the exact same feeling I had when I got sober: I wanted a better life more than I wanted to stay the same. I was in a whole new arena of willingness that I'd never known before. I entered a new world of acceptance I'd never felt before.

The year after mom's death was a year of true transformation for me. After that realization, I changed my thoughts and I never experienced any pain or suffering around food or in life again!

KIDDING!

JK, JK.

In a lot of books and movies and other people's stories, it feels like there's this one magical moment and their life changed, BAM. They were fixed. But that isn't how it went for me.

I went to treatment again. Yup. AGAIN. I sound lighthearted, but I think that's a coping mechanism. I didn't want to tell you I went back again; I wish that my story was "and everything was easy and happily ever after" but it wasn't. I thought the last time I went to treatment was the hardest, but nope, it was this one. It was the same rehab I went to when I was sixteen, which wasn't very good during that time either, but I just needed *something*. I was now in my late twenties, working, in a relationship, doing all the normal life stuff, and I couldn't get it together . . . still. As I write this, I wonder how much of me went for eating disorder help and how much of me went to just get a fucking break from life.

I mean, listen, I was definitely IN my eating disorder at the time, but I was so used to it, it wasn't even that bad to me. But then when I think about my life, I mean sheesh, it was also pretty darn good! Sure, my mom had just died, and yes, my relationship wasn't that great at the time, and yes, I was in a job I didn't like, and yes, I was bingeing my brains out, but compared to so many other people and their situations, it was easy living!

But I had reached the point of not knowing what else to do but knowing I was so damn tired of it. And let me tell you, staying in treatment did not "fix me."

That's what I had wanted for so long. I wanted someone to fix me. So I'd reach for whatever could alleviate the pain the fastest. Food, booze, dating, shopping, you name it. And guess what? That shit never lasts. It's fun in the moment, but you're always left with you.

In treatment, even this last round, I never learned how to think differently. I never learned how to actually change my behaviors or hang out in emotional discomfort without scrambling to cover it up with busyness. I never really did that deep work. Even with my best intentions, that last trip to treatment was like all the others, a Band-Aid on a gushing wound.

So, naturally, even out of treatment, I kept repeating the same patterns. It was like waking up in *Groundhog Day*.

But eventually, I found a way to begin closing the wound from the inside.

CHAPTER 8:

FIX ME

There was a woman I'd been following online for about six years. I got her emails, in which she often shared her own experiences with food and life. She didn't shove the normal "just stop eating when you are full!" or "have you thought about going for a walk or taking a bath instead of eating?" and "follow this thirty-day plan to end binge eating and lose weight for good" that you typically hear which made me want to throw up and not just because I was a die-hard bulimic. She was different. I trusted her without knowing her. She wasn't constantly showing her body half-naked and never talked about intentional weight loss. I felt like she got me. So I hired her. She was the first coach I ever hired. She told me what I'm sure other people had said before, but for some reason, hearing it from her really clicked: "You really need to rest."

I needed permission to rest. I needed her to tell me, over and over, "It's okay to do nothing. It's okay to eat food. It's okay not to work out." I needed to know that someone else "got it." I wanted help from someone I thought was inspiring and had a life going for herself, but who understood the insanity in my brain.

We talked twice a month, and when I signed up to work with her, I made a serious commitment to myself. *Renae, you're going to want to binge. You're going to want to purge. You're going to want to push yourself. You're going to want to quit. Plan on all of that happening and keep going.*

Here's where the highs and lows come in. With food especially, there isn't a clear line in the sand of "and then I never ate 'too much' again." Or "From that day on, I never had negative body image thoughts or compared myself to another person again." It doesn't work like that.

You still have to eat. You still have to live and be a human. That never clicked for me before.

For so many of those prior attempts, I was still essentially dieting. I still had a clear idea in my head of what the "right" amount of food was or what "enough" of something looked like and what *I* should look like. So every time I had one bite too many, one extra cookie, or got a little too full, it threw me right back into the cycle, year after year. I realized I had to completely change my relationship to food and my body in a way that I never had in the past.

I gave it a go.

My normal time for a binge was 3:00 to 4:00 p.m. or in the evening. One night, I had a dinner reservation. My routine for going out to dinner was to eat as little as possible beforehand so I could eat whatever I wanted without guilt at the meal. But I was hungry, and it was midafternoon. *Okay, I can have a snack, it's fine. I can actually eat food before I go out to a nice dinner. It is okay.*

While I had that snack, I was very careful. I was overly mindful of how much I was eating; I didn't want to have too much. I didn't want to ruin my dinner. But all that pressure added more stress, and that additional stress made me . . . eat. What was supposed to be just a little something to hold me over for an hour and a half ended up being basically a full meal. I was stuffed!

Now I can't go to dinner. Now I can't eat. Should I just binge? Should I purge so I can eat what I want? What excuse can I think of to get out of this reservation? There is no way I can go out to eat after eating all of that.

The usual thoughts swirled around my mind.

NO.

I am going. I know exactly what will happen if I stay home alone. I know how those tapes play out, and they never end well. I will think I am going to stay home to stay "safe." I will feel bad for bailing on my plans and I will binge. It has happened countless times. I am doing something different. I am going and I am eating dinner.

I arrived at that restaurant full. I arrived still tasting the snack I had ninety minutes earlier on my breath. I ordered myself a meal at that fancy-ass restaurant and ate what I wanted and boxed up the rest.

And the next day, I woke up and the world was still spinning. I was hungry again.

Everything was fine.

I had never done something like that. I had never sat through that kind of fullness; I had never ordered a meal after eating a snack (turned meal), then gone home and gone to bed.

Proud is an understatement of how I felt. Over the next year, I had so many more moments like that.

None of this was brand new to me because I'd gone through waves of similar experiences in previous years. Every year building up to this one had strengthened me and taught me things I couldn't see at the time. None of what I'd gone through in the past was a waste. Trying all the plans and programs, going to twelve-step groups, working with trainers and meal plans, signing up for weight watching, going on Whole30, and experiencing the lowest of the lows that arrived after each of those failed attempts—it was all setting me up for where I was now: feeling stable about food and my body, focused on work, starting my own business, exercising, eating well, and enjoying life.

But sometimes you can get a little cocky, and the universe lets you know what's up . . .

MAYBE I SHOULD COUNT MACROS NOW

I'd been following this other person on Instagram. She worked with women around macros and "helping you look good naked." I was drawn to her. She didn't seem like a ding-dong fitness influencer; she was smart, funny, and had what I thought was a pretty balanced approach to food. And she had a banging body.

Maybe I should count macros now, I thought. *I mean, I feel great around food, and abs would be nice. You know, just a little tighter and more lean.*

I hired her. Her job was to help me mold and craft my body into a shape I found more ideal: to lose fat, gain muscle, and create all the shapes and curves every woman wants. It was exhilarating, thinking about this new body. The idea of a bit of hunger, a touch of restraint - sacrificing some of the culinary joys for a stronger, leaner me—it all felt thrilling... with just a sprinkle of doubt. *Are you really sure about this?* I'd fought hard to reach peace with food and my body, so I struck a bargain with myself: *if it gets too tough, I bow out.*

Fast forward two months, and I hit a wall. *Wow, I can't do this.*

The first month was okay. I weighed and measured myself regularly and tracked everything I ate (oh the mind numbing monotony!). Though I wasn't new to this game—and frankly, never a fan—I was swept up by the excitement of imagining a transformed me. It was actually working! The scale nudged down. Each week, I'd send swimsuit snaps to my trainer to track changes. Day thirty-five? There was a noticeable difference. Small, sure, but enough to stoke my motivation. This isn't for nothing, I thought. All was going to plan, except...

I didn't feel the surge of confidence I craved. I didn't relax into a more comfortable life. Quite the opposite—I saw food reduced to mere numbers again. I ignored my body's cues, opting instead for what an app dictated I could eat. My body fixation grew; I worried about missing a workout and losing ground.

Damn . . . I guess I can't do this. But really, I could do it. I could have kept tracking and weighing and doing all the things, but the cost of it all wasn't worth it anymore. So I stopped.

Just because you *can* doesn't mean you *should*—it doesn't mean the doing is worth it.

This was the first time since I was a teenager that I could see what was happening and *stepped away* without massive intervention.

Weighing myself, meticulously tracking every meal, and snapping weekly photos of my progress—it just wasn't worth it. Not worth my sanity, not worth my sense of freedom, not worth my energy. Yet, I found myself drawn back into the fray. The diet industry's voice is overpowering. The norm is to alter your body, so much so that a woman proclaiming, "I'm not dieting and I love my body," can leave others agape. Sometimes, there's even a murmur of resentment because you don't feel that confidence, and instead, you feel miserable.

The diet industry has become more cunning over time. It's revamped its language, marketing strategies, and tactics to reel you in. If you find yourself being pulled back in, resist the urge to blame yourself. When thoughts like, "Maybe I should eliminate flour and sugar. Those people look fantastic, and it seems effective for them," creep in, remember those influencers are likely profiting from your participation in their plans—and it's not your fault. These promoters of thinness as the ultimate solution are living under the same societal pressures as you, susceptible to the same crafty marketing and pervasive cultural messages. Yes, the dominant myth that 'thin is supreme' is widespread, but remember, there is hope. There is a path to break free from this cycle.

A NEW RELATIONSHIP TO FOOD AND BODY

There is this idea that once we set a goal, it should just happen. Quickly. In our minds there's a path that makes perfect sense, it's crystal clear, and it's the right way to go. But 99.9 percent of the time, things don't go this way. The failures, the setbacks, the belief that we're "undoing all we worked for" is actually the process.

No one has a path without failure. No one takes a journey during which they don't wonder if any of it is even working. Every "relapse" I had, I thought I was failing. I turned every setback into proof that my goal was never going to happen for me. I couldn't see at the time that it was actually ALL happening. That I hadn't "undone" anything, I was just doing it. I didn't realize that it was during the moments of struggle I was learning the most. Sometimes we need to go back to what we used to do to really solidify and remember we don't want to do it anymore. Sometimes it takes a couple trips around the same block for the truth to sink in.

That IS the process.

When I look back through this timeline of events, there were so many months when I felt like I wasn't making any progress. Months where I felt like nothing was working and I'd be stuck forever, but now I can see that the process was happening. Just because we can't see it in the moment, does not mean it isn't happening.

After finally understanding I did NOT want to spend another five years of my life as a prisoner to food scales, weight scales, or what my stomach looked like when I stood sideways in the mirror, I committed to letting myself eat. I committed to unfollowing on social media the people I couldn't help but compare myself to and who made me feel inadequate. I committed to doing whatever it took.

And I did. Sometimes I ate more than I wanted. Sometimes I left half a sandwich on a plate because I thought I was full—only to discover that thirty minutes later I was hungry. Some days I bought two donuts, thinking I would give the second away, and ate them both. Some days I ate more chocolate than physically felt good. Some days I wanted the salad but got the burger—then felt like I needed to eat it to prove to myself I could eat whatever the hell I wanted.

This was my work. Getting comfortable with hunger *and* fullness. Realizing it's okay to get overly full. It is okay to go out to a meal and just order an appetizer and enjoy the company.

Understanding that I can get a burger and salad and fries if I need to. That it's okay to leave some meals wishing there was a little more. That it's okay to not fill my entire plate with vegetables.

That was my process: being really full and uncomfortable at times. Eating a few more rolls than

I expected. But also, comfortable eating salad and "healthy" things and realizing it wasn't restricting— that I truly enjoy those foods.

My decade and a half obsessing about food and my body, hating myself, pushing myself, and thinking I knew the "right way" to live really did a number on me—but also, in a way, it was the only thing that allowed me freedom. It was the only thing that allowed me to fully escape my thoughts and slow everything down. And if I was purging, no food in no quantity was off-limits.

I had to give myself the time to figure this out. To be curious and kind and not be in such a goddamn rush. WHICH IS NOT MY VIBE. I had to stop thinking I knew all the things all the time and just freakin' listen for once.

A NEW NORMAL

Some pivotal moments I experienced that you may understand as well. These are the "small" shifts and wins that "normal" people may not understand, but for anyone who has dealt with food stuff, you will get it. These are things I experienced that left me feeling a sense of pride in myself and the work I had done that is almost too hard to explain.

1. Eating dinner without three-quarters of my plate being vegetables. Like Cajun food, pasta, a grilled cheese.
2. Leaving food on my plate.
3. Forgetting there was ice cream in the freezer.
4. Eating cereal.
5. Not comparing myself to every woman in the room.
6. Resting when I'm tired.
7. Leaving a workout when I'm not feeling it.
8. Buying a bigger size of underwear.
9. Eating dessert in the middle of the day.
10. Boxing up my leftovers and not eating them with my bare hands on the drive home.
11. Seeing fast-food restaurants and knowing I don't have to binge there anymore.
12. Eating a salad that's actually satisfying and not just lettuce for volume.
13. Saying no to dessert.
14. Sharing food.
15. Finding comfort around other women.
16. Throwing food away.
17. Looking forward to things other than eating or food.
18. Recognizing myself in the mirror again.
19. Being able to go out to eat anywhere without fear.

LIVING WITHOUT THE CHAOS
AND CONSTANT CHATTER

When I think back to my previous life, it was absolute mayhem. I was drinking to oblivion and waking up with a wrecked car wondering how that happened, if anyone was hurt, and how I got home. I'd hit two or three fast-food restaurants, one right after the other, bingeing and purging for hours, knowing where every single restroom was. When I grocery shopped, I'd cram down two or three donuts and never pay for them. I bought tons of cakes, cookies, and candy and lied to the cashier about it being for a party, then ate it in the parking lot. I planned my relationships around working out. Burning off calories was always front and center. I wanted to be the best in the workout class, and I was always trying to move toward some kind of promotion at work. I never sat down, I never rested, I was always doing. I was always lying about something: where I was, what I ate, or how I felt.

I look back, and it's no wonder I sucked at school and relationships.

I had no idea how to not be in the tornado. I had no idea how to just have a normal night around a fire pit and chat. I didn't know what it was like to just linger and play games after a dinner party or enjoy a low-key afternoon with an easy walk and reading. I'd never done it.

My life, while privileged and wonderful in so many ways, was always moving in a cycle of chaos: booze, food, body, relationships, exercise . . . I had no practice living a normal life and no experience living with calm. The quiet was terrifying to me.

But I firmly believe that we have the power to transform any aspect of ourselves. However, change crawls at a maddeningly slow pace—it's like waiting for water to boil when you're starving. It really sucks. Yet, just because it's slow doesn't mean it's not in motion.

If you relate to this angst and anxiety, this inability to relax, know this: it's very common.

Food is the symptom. Food is the lowest hanging fruit. Our weight is the easiest thing to blame. But these are not the cause. Food is the manifestation of all our anxiety and control issues. This is how we soothe ourselves. This is one of the reasons why solely changing what you eat, losing weight, or eliminating food groups never gets to the core of our issues or works long term.

As you now know, I tried every single way I could think of to "fix" myself, to achieve a body I loved. All I wanted was to feel "normal" but every attempt left me feeling worse. I was unknowingly striving for perfection. Which, surprise surprise, is an impossible target to hit! For years I believed that if I could just attain perfection with my food, everything else would be fine.

And you have probably been doing this too. Staying on track for a few days or weeks only to fall off. Feeling great with your weight loss and then, "Damnit! How did I gain this all back?" Thinking it's going to be a great day but then someone brings donuts into work, and you know the second you can sneak in the break room, you are shoving four in your piehole as fast as possible.

So how on earth do you change? How do you achieve some freakin' **PEACE** around the donuts? Some trust with your body?

You aren't trying to win any fitness competitions, but damn, it would be nice to relax in the evening without eating your face off, to not hate your body, or to enjoy a burger at a cookout without guilt.

You're in luck, because the next section is going to show you exactly how to create this change for yourself.

PART 2:

RELIEF

CHAPTER 9:
WHY CHANGE SUCKS

I hope to hell you haven't been in the shit as deep as I was. Or if you have, that you're out of it now. (If you're still in it, there's a list of resources at the back for you.) But this is for you if you see something of yourself in my desperation to escape reality, in finding it hard to stop and sit with yourself. If you find emotional comfort in food and drink, don't trust yourself, or are living a life that looks good but doesn't *feel* right. These are the most essential ideas I learned the hard way, the mindset shifts that have helped my clients, and the first questions you can ask yourself to start these shifts in your own life.

Before we get started, I want to set the stage a little bit.

This work is not a diet, this work is not a few little tips, tricks, or secrets. This is an identity shift.

You are going to be looking at yourself, your thoughts, and situations in your life in a way you never thought possible, and there are times it is going to get uncomfortable. There are times you are going to want to kick me in the throat and burn this book. You are going to think this is never going to work for you and wonder why you are even trying.

Know that this is not a sign you need to quit. This is a sign of doing something different. And when you do something different you can get a different result, which is why you are here, right?

Odds are, if I told you to just follow a meal plan, hit a new set of macros, or list out all the ways you need to improve, you would be pretty comfortable with that, right?

Yeah. This is not that.

We are going to radically change your relationship with food and your body and ultimately yourself.

You are here because you have spent years, if not decades, at war with yourself. It is as if your brain is on one planet and your body is on the other. And when YOU, your single self, are at war with yourself, or are that disconnected from yourself, it is impossible to make the progress you want.

Through our time together, we are going to challenge old beliefs, eliminate behaviors that aren't serving you, and get clear on this next version of you.

This is the mental process almost every single client I have ever worked with has gone through:

1. This sounds too good to be true. I don't think I can do this. I am pretty sure I am the only person this won't work for, but I am going to try it.
2. This is amazing! This all makes so much sense. I am feeling good!
3. This is terrible. I hate this.
4. I don't think this is working. I think I am going backward. I don't think I will ever figure this out.
5. OOOOOH. I GET IT!
6. Whoa. I can't believe how far I have come in such a short period of time! I am so glad I did this.

If you notice, steps three and four both suck. And this is when a lot of people are like, "NOPE! I am going back to my old ways, BYEEEEE!"

But if you stay . . . If you dig in and trust me and trust the process and know that the discomfort WILL end, you will get to the other side.

HABITS AND CHANGE

With every fiber in your body, doing something different, a.k.a. change, will feel like running into oncoming traffic.

Until it doesn't. And then that change is your new normal.

When I stopped bingeing and obsessing over grams of carbs in bread or meticulously studying menus before going out to eat, I felt like I was going to claw out of my own skin. I felt like I was doing something wrong. And also, logically, I knew it was the right thing to do. Talk about a wild ride of emotions.

Part of me was screaming, *Don't do it*, and the other part of me was screaming, *Just do it!* But the less you feed the old ways, the weaker they get.

It's kind of like feeding stray cats. Let me explain.

It starts out harmless, right? One cute little kitty is there, you see her sweet eyes and think, *Oh, that poor thing! I will just leave a few scraps out for her.* Three days later, there's another cat, and you think, *Hmm okay, she must have told her friend. I guess that's okay, but just this one time! I am stopping tomorrow.* Then you blink and there are seventeen cats at your back door demanding food immediately, and you realize you're in way over your head but also that you can't turn back!

So what do you do?

You stop feeding the damn cats. And for the first few days and weeks, it hurts like hell. The cats are loud. The cats are cute. Your heart is breaking, and you feel like a horrible person as you see them begin to taper off, and you fear they'll die without you. Your days are consumed with thoughts of the cats.

But two months later, you come home from work and realize there are no cats! There are none of those fuzzy little fuckers running around meowing and demanding food or clawing at your pant leg. You can walk inside and rest with zero guilt! Huh! Imagine that!

The cats also learned and did something different.

They were hungry and looking for food. They found a place that was readily handing out food—problem solved. When the food stopped coming in, they hung around for a little while to see if that would change. The food kept not coming in, so the cats changed locations and found food elsewhere.

Just as the cats moved on when their expectations weren't met, we too face similar disillusionment in our lives. Often, we are lured by the promise of immediate and dramatic transformations. You have been fed wild before-and-after pictures (body, career, skin, hair, energy, etc.) that when you go through your own process of change, well, frankly, it will be pretty anticlimactic and definitely not photo-worthy. You will think it's not working or it's not working fast enough. But really, all those other people are liars. Think about growing your hair out. First off, the process is freaking terrible, I think we can all agree on that! But it's like nothing is happening for the longest time; then one day, you look in the mirror and think, *Wow! My hair is finally at the length I want!* Think of it from another point of view: if you haven't seen a friend for seven months and you finally meet up, you notice how long her hair has gotten but she hasn't because she has been looking at it every day.

Without those teeny, tiny changes in your hair getting just a smidge longer every day, you never would have grown it out five inches. And during that time, you may have gotten it trimmed a few times to keep it looking healthy. So it isn't that you were going backward in your journey of growing your hair out, you were taking the necessary steps to get the best hair.

Creating change in your own life isn't a straight line up, which I am sure you have heard a hundred times, but we need to hear this over and over. Sometimes we have to go back a little to move forward faster.

You need to pull back on how much you are doing, how hard you are working, and all your efforts so you can do it right. Making any change first comes with knowing what we are doing and what needs changed.

Because you can't change something you are unaware of. And if you are like many people on the planet, you are on autopilot in most areas of your life. Existing entirely in fight or flight or so used to doing or thinking something a certain way that an option of doing it differently never once occurred to you. You aren't conscious of the choices you are making. So to begin your own process of change, you have to start here:

Try This: Awareness as the First Step Toward Change
Over the next three days—notice your own thoughts, behaviors, and choices.

Jot it down in your phone, write it in your journal, email it to yourself; just get it down. Throughout your day, pay attention to exactly what and how you are doing and what you are thinking. You will be shocked at what you discover when you do this.

For example:

- I immediately tore my body apart when I looked in the mirror.
- I spent thirty minutes looking at people online that I was jealous of.
- I ordered the same lunch I always get, and I didn't even like the taste of it.
- I never realized how mad I was at my coworker.
- I spent my entire morning panicked with racing thoughts about the day.
- I went to take a nap and the whole time I was beating myself up about taking a nap.
- The whole time I was eating my meal I was telling myself how fat I was.
- Turns out, I am very annoyed at my parent.
- Etc.

When you start to see what you are doing and you look at it in a nonjudgmental way, this is when you can do something different. And this is going to be pivotal in changing your relationship to food and your body.

Because you will want to immediately beat yourself up about it, shame yourself, or go into guilt mode. Resist the temptation! None of that will be helpful here. Be as unbiased and neutral as possible. All that is happening is you are having a series of thoughts about some things. That's it. You are just having some sentences move through your brain.

When you remove the emotion, it becomes infinitely easier to change.

The real miracle is going out to lunch and realizing you didn't tally up all the calories in your head. It's going to bed and realizing not once did you have the desire to binge. It's trying on clothes that look terrible on you and tossing them to the side without having a meltdown. It's thinking that ice cream sounds good and eating some ice cream. It's hearing a friend talk about her workout and not immediately making it mean you aren't working out enough.

It is a process. It is a shedding of all your old ideas, habits, and routines. It is letting go of the thought patterns that you used for years and replacing them with ones that move you in the direction you want to be going.

And then, one day on a random Tuesday at dinner while lasagna is being served, you think, *Wow. I can't believe this. I can just sit down and eat lasagna. And bread. And not lose my mind.*

PERMISSION TO EXIST

In this process, you give yourself permission to be an imperfect human.

Let's take a moment to admit just how damn hard it is to go easy on ourselves.

(If you need to cue up Adele's "Easy On Me" and play it on repeat for the remainder of the book, I fully support that decision.)

As we begin to loosen our grip on food, we begin to trust ourselves more. And when we begin to trust ourselves, we let out a breath we had no idea we were holding—for years, if not decades. We start to realize our lives are about so much more than a pant size or calories consumed in a day. It's so easy to look at thin women and assume they're happy and #thriving. There is a huge difference, and feeling in your body, between "successfully restricting" and truly living freely around food.

On my podcast, *Ditch The Binge*, I did an interview with a former client, Kendra, and she said, "Not only am I trusting myself more around food, but in all areas of my life." She was making stronger and faster decisions, comparing herself less, and not spinning out for days or weeks over what the "right" thing to do was or regretting a choice she had made.

It may not be as clear now if you are actively struggling with binge or emotional eating, or flipping between doing good and eating your face off at night, how attempting to constantly control your food, dieting, and then going off the rails (which is a normal side effect of dieting/restricting) impacts the trust you have with yourself and the confidence you feel within yourself.

I was a successful restrictor for a while. I was able to keep the perfect meal plan, I'd have workout streaks when nothing could stop me. I was "committed." But in reality, I was running on adrenaline and fear. I'd wake up and work out not because I felt empowered but because I felt terrified of what would happen if I didn't.

I didn't eat salads and heap on the vegetables because I loved the taste and wanted to feel good in my body; I did it because I was starving and needed the volume to smother my hunger, so I wouldn't gain weight. My life was still shackled to my weight, driven by anxiety.

I was still terrified of food, weight, and not getting my workout in. It wasn't an easy way to live, but it was consistent. Being consumed with food, weight, and exercise was consistent. I never had to be with me. And thank god because I had no idea HOW to. When I just tried being alone with myself, I felt like my skin would melt off.

But I got to the point where running from myself was no longer working either. Which could be where you are at as well.

Learning to trust myself and be with myself was surprisingly hard because it sounds so easy!

Now, with hindsight, I suppose it isn't that surprising. I mean, from the age of fifteen, fitness magazines filled my innocent brain with the idea that how my body looks was THE most important thing about me, pushing tips and tricks on how to eat as little as possible and deceive my body into ignoring its hunger.

That day after my mom died, when I decided, *No, fuck this, I'm done*, I was shocked at how quiet my brain started to feel—and also how uncomfortable it started to feel.

What do I do with all this time? Without hours of bingeing at night or exercising during the day—what do I do?

As cheesy as this is going to sound —that is part of the journey. You are literally recreating and reestablishing a relationship with yourself. You're getting to know this present-day version of you, not some interpretation of you from ten, fifteen, twenty years ago. It is the same process with which we build a relationship with anyone else: slow, steady, sometimes awkward, sometimes messy, and it's all okay.

Because you're a bad b*tch, and don't you forget it!

Phew, I just had to snap us out of the kumbayas. Really, though, you are.

When we spend our whole lives running from the truest version of ourselves, when we spend our whole lives trying to mold ourselves into some ideal human for someone else, we never get the utmost pleasure and freedom of experiencing life in our truest forms.

When we're trying to be someone we think other people want, when we're trying to control every last detail of our food and lives, it is exhausting and it feels chaotic and it occupies every waking moment.

I remember the first time I forgot what I ate for lunch while I was eating dinner. That might seem like a weird thing to recognize, but it was huge for me. I always based my dinner off what I ate for lunch. I decided what I could eat by analyzing everything I'd eaten earlier, never by what I was hungry for. In that moment, I realized I was finally listening to my body. I was trusting myself. I was more in my life than I was in my food. The food noise was getting quieter, and my obsession over every single thing I ate was diminishing. But here comes the annoying part that our brains do: I was also terrified because then I thought, *If I don't worry, obsess, count, or keep track of what I have eaten, I am never going to stop! I will never stop gaining weight.*

It turns out this is the most common fear people have. And it hasn't happened to me or anyone I've worked with. In fact, a common side effect of letting yourself eat what you want and listening to your body, is that you eat far less of your binge foods and in amounts you enjoy.

You may be thinking, "Listen, Renae, I like you, but this is crazy. You don't understand *my* type of eating. You don't understand how *I* operate. I will be the one person who keeps eating forever and ever. I am the person that cannot be trusted with chips in her house because once night time hits, all bets are off! How do I even deal with my stress or decompress without eating?!"

Keep reading. These next few chapters are for you.

CHAPTER 10:
WHAT'S KEEPING YOU STUCK

First, we are going to look at why you are doing the same things over and over again, not making the progress or change you want.

And then I'll tell you what you need to do to get out of them.

CONTROL

When we attempt to control our food (or anything really! The weather, our pets, our kids, other people) we will inevitably lose control—which you have probably discovered. Eventually, your body wins. Your hunger wins. Biology wins. It's common for our binges to happen in direct proportion to the degree to which you are restricting.

Believe it or not, there is zero evidence out there that a diet actually works long term.

None.

There is, however, a lot of evidence to prove diets *don't* work and ultimately make you gain weight. A diet isn't just a name-brand fad that's floating around. A diet is a way of *thinking*. It is the "good, bad, right, wrong" labels we put on food. When you look at food in this light, it is like the trigger that spirals you into polishing off that bag of chips or sneaking back into the kitchen for the ninth time even though you aren't hungry and it no longer tastes good anymore, but "What's the point? I've already ruined today! Might as well REALLY ruin it!"

Anytime you attach morality to food, you become its prisoner.

For example, the times you eat more than you want: you have four cookies instead of one, you start snackin' on TJ's dried mango but then look down and realize you ate the whole damn bag (seriously though, I'm deeply offended those are supposed to be more than one serving). During those times, you didn't do anything wrong. You just ate more food. That's it.

This does not mean all food is good for you all the time no matter what.

This means food is just food.

Eat a head of broccoli.

Eat four donuts.

You are still a good person.

You aren't hurting babies, puppies, or one of those a-holes that can't seem to understand how to use a blinker.

You just ate food.

Eating four donuts doesn't make you bad, you haven't done anything wrong. In the same way that eating a head of broccoli doesn't make you superior. (You will probably have raunchy gas though.)

In both cases, you ate food. The end. That's it.

Name-brand diets were never my thing. Yes, I tried Whole30, WeightWatchers, Atkins, South Beach, and so on, but mostly I had my own idea of what my food should look like. I, like many others, was a walking, talking encyclopedia of knowledge about calories, nutrition information, the best and worst things to eat on a menu, and so on.

Diets do create changes . . . *in the beginning*. Think back to the first time you went on a diet. It was probably easy and maybe even a little fun. And you likely had some success too! It isn't uncommon to see quick changes and be able to sustain them for a few months, maybe a year—some may make it to three years—but inevitably, you can't adhere to it the way you once did. The results you saw and the feelings you had from that first diet are something you keep chasing after but can't seem to grab. And you lose control.

This is your "dieting rebound," which is basically when you binge your face off after a period of restriction. It feels almost as if you're making up for lost time.

Okay, so what the hell are you supposed to eat?

Another thing that happens when you plan on losing weight, going on a diet, or getting back on track tomorrow is "last supper mentality"—the feast before the famine.

And you can go through this phase many, many times. Here's an example of just one time I did:

In an exhausting night of eating everything in my house with the only light coming from the glow of my computer screen, I typed in the search bar, "Am I addicted to food?"

And that was when I found a twelve-step meeting specifically for this! I read over the site and dug deeper into this program. Everything that was there was ME! *THIS IS WHAT I HAVE BEEN LOOKING FOR! This is the thing that will fix me!*

I was relieved! I finally found it. I was finally going to get the help and guidance I needed! I looked up the schedule and found a meeting that I could attend, and it was just a couple of days away.

Despite feeling both relief and excitement that I had discovered a solution to end my food-related chaos, my eating habits took an unexpected turn for the worse in the following days. It was as if my appetite had declared a full-scale rebellion, defying all reason and restraint, which I didn't think was possible. I cleared out all the day-old pastries at coffee shops—shoving them into my laptop bag which was brought along solely for this purpose, pretending not to notice the strange look on the cashier's face. Any crumb of self-control was gone. I was hitting up Taco Bell and McDonald's, and raiding discount racks at grocery stores, buying and eating anything and everything my eyes came across or my mind desired. And it was during all this I was further convincing myself how badly I needed this twelve-step program and that it would be the thing to lay all this madness to rest.

However, it wasn't that I was any more out of control around food. It wasn't that I needed the group more than ever because my food was getting worse. The whole reason my eating went from pretty terrible to wildly unrestrained in a way that knew no bounds, was the anticipation of the new program. I knew two cheeseburgers, a large fry, and large McFlurry likely weren't on "the plan." I knew the freedom to eat an entire peach pie wouldn't be on the list of "acceptable snacks." So I'd better get it all in now! I'd better eat everything I want and then some because I am not doing it once I start that program—a.k.a., last supper mentality.

It wasn't the food making me binge; it was the fear of food being taken away.

TWO FORMS OF RESTRICTION

Most people think food restriction is solely physical, like not eating enough calories. That is certainly one form of restriction, and that is the one that must be addressed first. If you aren't eating enough food, you WILL be obsessed and preoccupied with thoughts of food or feel out of control around food—the end. If you don't already know about the Minnesota Starvation Study, I encourage you to read about it.

The first and most important step to end binge eating and stop thinking about food all day long is to *eat enough*. If you are like most of the women I have worked with, you will try to tell me you are eating enough, and you will honestly believe it. And I say this with love, but you aren't. Most of the women I work with significantly undereat, then wonder why they binge in the evenings. If you don't get enough food in the first half of the day, you *will* get enough in the second half of the day one way or another. I don't care what your favorite fitness influencer eats. I don't care that some people claim to exist on a single grain of rice and feel like they have enough energy for hours because they have trained their body how to metabolize carbs in a new way or whatever bullshit they are saying. You can't not eat and expect your body to be like "Oh okay, yeah! No problem!" That isn't how it works. You gotta eat. Okay, I think I have officially hit that point home. Ha!

So maybe you aren't quite falling into the extreme of last supper mentality.

You don't feel like you are restricting, you feel like you eat pretty healthy for the most part, buuuut every time you eat a chip, candy bar, or cookie, you can't stop. You go back for more.

What gives?

Even if you're eating "enough" calories, like doing paleo or hitting your macros, you're still restricting. You may not be *physically* restricting, and you may be eating plenty, but there is a second, very sneaky type of restriction that personally had me in a choke hold for years.

If you're certain you are eating enough food but *still* find yourself unable to stop at one cookie or sneaking into the kitchen after dark, this is the culprit. This is the thing keeping you in the cycle.

And this *thing* is "mental restriction."

Let me give you an example:

You've been wanting something sweet and finally decide to let yourself have the cookie.

It's fine! I have been eating really good. One cookie is very reasonable. I am just going to sit down and eat this like a normal person.

But once you start eating the cookie, the anxiety sets in. The whole time, all you are doing is thinking about how unhealthy it is, how bad it is, how it is undoing all your hard work, or how after you finish this you are *never* going to buy it again.

You are telling yourself that what you are doing is bad and won't be repeated. This also signals "Get it all in now because after this, NO MORE!"

Your body is responding in a natural way. When we face any sort of restriction, we panic and stock up immediately. It isn't that you're out of control or addicted—you're simply responding to deprivation. Or the thought of deprivation.

Think about the last binge you had or the last time you felt out of control around food. Did you enjoy what you were eating? Were you savoring it? Were you telling yourself, "This is so good and if I want more later, I will have some"? Or was it something more along the lines of, "I shouldn't be doing this. This is going to make me fat. I might as well finish it because I am never buying it again!"

If you identify with the second experience, then you, my friend, are living a life of restriction, and that is the number one reason for binge eating.

For you to achieve freedom around food, to trust your body, to not feel out of control, complete allowance—physical and mental—is crucial. I want to hit this point hard because this was the exact thing that kept me bingeing and feeling unable to stop eating once I started for a long, long time and may be happening for you too.

In your head, you are telling yourself what the "right" amount to eat is, what "enough" should look like, and what a "normal" person would eat. The problem is that this idea of "enough" is skewed by years of dieting or consuming inaccurate information in *Shape* magazine, the online macro calculator, or wherever else you were deciding what you should be allowed to eat. So the moment you eat over what you think is acceptable, that is when the binge begins. You go into all-or-nothing thinking and tell yourself, "I've messed up my day's food, so I will start again tomorrow," keeping you in the cycle.

Go big or go home, amiright?

"Listen, Renae, I AM eating too much! I will eat an entire bag of chips! I will do two full lines of Oreos!"

I hear you.

AND . . .

Even if it *was* "too much," even if it *was* "bad," guess what? Knowing something was too much, bad, not good for you, etc.—has it ever stopped you from eating? I know it sure as hell never stopped me! I didn't think a box of graham crackers and tub of frosting was "healthy." But when I would slip into panic, stress, and mental restriction, what would have been like eight graham crackers and some frosting went to eating it until it was gone.

By *allowing* the food and reminding myself over and over that this is JUST food, that I am allowed to eat, that I am not doing anything wrong—that this is OKAY—the desire to eat the all of everything started to lessen. Over time there were more and more days when I didn't want to eat so much I felt sick. There was more space between my binges, and they became less aggressive.

What you are doing isn't working. The shame, the limits on amounts, the trying to get it perfect, it isn't working. So what *will* work?

CHAPTER 11:

GETTING OFF THE WHEEL, ONE THOUGHT AND DECISION AT A TIME.

Now that we have covered why nothing has worked long term, let's get into what you really want to know: how to get over this food stuff for good!

INTUITIVE EATING HAS ENTERED THE CHAT

So what the hell do you eat?

When you have spent most of your life relying on a meal plan, app, or some kind of calculator to let you know what you can or cannot eat, "just eat" feels damn near impossible. Which is annoying, right? I used to look at kids eating food and get so frustrated that they could just eat. They knew what they wanted, they stopped with half their grilled cheese and chips left on their plate, took one bite of cookie, and moved on.

How can a seven-year-old do this and I can't?

The frustration is real, AND . . . you can get there too. This is where "intuitive eating" comes in.

The idea behind intuitive eating is to reconnect your mind and your body by tuning back into your body's cues.

Your body *wants* you to feel good. You are designed to know how to eat. At one point you did trust yourself. The problem is, you are tirelessly kicked in the gut with messages from diet culture and society telling you, reminding you, never giving you a second to forget that you are not okay as you are. You need to look smaller, be more toned, be more muscular, more feminine, more successful, happier, be in better relationships, make more money, and on and on and on.

So, you begin to diet. Harmlessly and hopefully.

Hopeful that this is what will bring comfort in your skin. The love and happiness in your life. The fulfillment you have been seeking.

But what this actually does is push you further away from everything you truly want. It creates more tension and distrust within you. Because you now begin questioning yourself even more.

"I want the turkey sandwich, but I have been reading about carbs and how bad they are, so I will have a breadless sandwich."

This seems kind of harmless. Like, "Okay cool, no bread, big deal." It is much deeper than this though.

Your relationship with food and body is often a mirror for how you are feeling in the rest of your life.

It is not a coincidence that the majority of the women I work with almost all say, "I want to trust myself more. I want to stop caring what other people think."

You lost that trust with yourself over the years. You had it, at one point, and you gave it away.

But you are here because we are getting it back!

I went through it too. This is exactly what happened to me as a teenager. I didn't feel good enough, I felt like an outsider, and I began dieting—in the simplest terms. That led to completely overriding all my internal cues.

When I was hungry, I didn't eat. When I craved something that was "bad," I shoved it to the side and ate something "good." I consumed low-calorie foods to get the feeling of being full, but I wasn't—I cut the cord between my brain and body. I got a sense of superiority and purpose from it in the beginning, but that quickly faded. It didn't take long for me to dislike and distrust myself even more.

Given all the information we have about how diets don't work long term and how much more they screw us up than help us, it is unbelievable that diets are still so prevalent and prescribed. Now, however, they're masked as wellness plans, "healthy eating," or services, like Noom.

Or WeightWatchers . . . err, wait, what's their latest rebrand? I can't keep track.

Diet plans, meal plans, programs, points—these are all external forces, all pushing you away from yourself and preventing you from listening to your body. Which is why eating when you're hungry, stopping when full, and knowing what you truly enjoy eating feel pretty damn hard to do. These answers have not been based off what your body desires but what your mind demands.

I remember the first time I ordered exactly what I wanted off the menu. I remember not having to stay in the salad section. I remember scrolling through the whole thing in it's entirety thinking, *I can have whatever I want.*

It was SO FREEING!

My client Laurie experienced an "I CANNOT BELIEVE THIS IS HAPPENING!" moment relating to intuitive eating with leftovers:

I went out to lunch with a friend; we opted for Mexican food, which I can do now, and the chips and salsa situation don't even freak me out anymore. I ordered what I wanted and realized about three-quarters of the way through that I was done. I *could* have finished it all with just a few more bites and a little determination, but I didn't want it. I didn't feel like I *had* to. I was satisfied. I got the rest to go in a box to eat later.

I never have leftovers! I always wanted to be the person that got to have leftovers, but leaving food on my plate made me extremely anxious. I felt like I had to eat it all, no matter how full I was. Being able to not only eat at a restaurant that used to be completely off-limits but not leave it so full I felt sick blew my mind. It seems silly to feel proud of yourself for doing something like leaving four bites of a burrito or not eating two baskets of chips, but I was!

If you have dieted or tried to lose weight, it has been drilled into your head that there is a right and wrong way to eat. That there are clearly defined right and wrong amounts of food and right and wrong times to eat it. That way of thinking and constantly trying to "get it right" is just another form of restriction and will keep you from ever really "getting it."

Coming from the land of harsh rules and clearly defined amounts, jumping into intuitive eating can feel like jumping off a plane without a parachute.

So we will ease into it.

First off, intuitive eating is not something you can get wrong. Try to let go of the idea that you can do this perfectly.

And for you type A perfectionists, this is going to be one of the hardest parts. It is actually super easy, but your brain is not going to want to let that be the case.

I hear from women all the time "Am I doing this right?" when we are working through this section of the process.

And this usually comes after a day where they ate more Sour Patch Kids than they expected, they decided to order the salad and skip the fries, or they ate a meal that sounded good but wouldn't be what they would normally eat.

And the answer is often yes.

There will be days where you eat a lot of food and others not so much.

Days when you eat a salad for lunch and other days you are freakin' *hungry* and have two breakfasts before 9:00 a.m. and seconds at dinner.

All of it is okay.

But you don't hear this message.

You see the graphs and charts of perfectly portioned food.

"Four ounces protein, half a cup of rice, half your plate with veggies, and one ounce of dark chocolate." NOOOOOOO!!!

It has been drilled into your mind that 1) this is enough food, 2) this is how your food should look all the time, and 3) this boring-ass meal should satisfy you.

We are slowly going to be eradicating that nonsense out of your mind.

And remember, learning about and incorporating intuitive eating is just one tiny tool in the whole process, okay? How you eat and exist around food the first few weeks and first few months will look a whole lot different six months later.

So how do you begin to bring your mind and body closer together again and start to reestablish that trust?

Try This: Learning Intuitive Eating

To get started, try to resist the urge to judge what you eat or want to eat. The goal is to just listen to your body. Your body knows better than any external source what it needs. Better than any calorie counter, macro plan, or system.

Next time you open the fridge to gather a meal or open a menu at a restaurant, pause. Try asking yourself these questions (or versions of them you discover work well for you):

"What sounds good to me right now? Something lighter or heavier? Something cold or hot?"

"Do I feel like some comfort food or maybe a lighter soup?"

If you find yourself scanning the menu for the lowest calorie option or ordering based on how much exercise you got that day, I encourage you to pause again and return to these new questions.

WHY INTUITIVE EATING FAILS MOST PEOPLE

Before you begin experimenting with intuitive eating, let me give you a heads up about what to look out for and why intuitive eating "fails" people.

Example: You are on vacation (or at a birthday party or out at a restaurant on a Tuesday night). You see your favorite dessert on the menu but just had the best dinner and aren't hungry. But this dessert looks *so* good! And it is your *favorite*!

You decide to eat it.

One of two things can happen here.

One: "Oh no! I am not hungry but ate the dessert! I have failed to intuitively eat. I can't get this right!" While eating the cake you are thinking of how many calories are in it, how you aren't really listening to your hunger, and that you have failed yet another thing.

Or two: You eat the cake. It was good. You weren't hungry. Now you are quite full. The end. This is *not* the "only eat when you are a certain number on the hunger scale" diet, which many people turn it into.

You WILL eat when you aren't hungry. You WILL eat past full.

You WILL emotionally eat.

Normal eaters do this.

You don't have to be a certain level of hunger to eat. You can just do it because it sounds good in the moment. There is no morality in what or how you eat. It is just food.

Sometimes you eat more and sometimes you eat less.

I CAN'T STOP EATING CARBS: LEGALIZATION

Intuitive eating, true "food freedom," cannot happen unless you are in complete allowance. Which takes us to legalization.

Shortly after you begin listening to your body and releasing the death grip of control you have had on your calories, macros, or eating perfectly, you will probably find yourself moving into the land of "legalization." Legalization is when you legalize, or allow, all foods.

You let yourself eat.

It is ordering the bagel sandwich instead of the lower carb option. It is wanting fries with your lunch, so you get the damn fries.

It is thinking ice cream sounds good, and instead of talking yourself out of it, you go get it.

It is craving carby, fatty, decadent food (and typically hardly any veggies or the "healthy" stuff) and letting yourself eat those things.

It is allowing all the foods.

You let yourself eat what you want.

And when you have been restricting carbs and or sugar or amounts of food, you will want more of those foods, and just more food overall, in the beginning.

It is kind if like reaching the tippy top point on a rollercoaster, right before you drop. You are excited, adrenaline is pulsing through you, but you are also kind of wondering if you are going to die in the next three seconds. What I am trying to say is it is fun and scary.

Legalization is kind of like the right of passage to true food freedom. This process can be an extremely freeing experience and terrifying; usually a mixture of both. I am hoping this section is going to help put your mind at ease about it.

I wasn't aware of legalization in this sense until about a year into my own recovery process, when I learned how so much of my own behavior made sense! "So *that's* why I was eating ice cream every single night!"

Kind of like when you spend all day crying, feeling exhausted, hating everyone, but also feeling alone and like everyone hates you and being certain life is over, and then you start your period.

You're probably thinking, "UHHHH. If I don't control my food, I will never stop eating and never stop gaining weight!" This is an understandable worry and a very common one, AND, I have yet to see this happen, in myself, my clients, or the countless other women I know who have done this work. I know you may fear being the *one* person it does happen to, and I hear you, I get it, I had the exact same thought; so does every other person I have worked with, but you have to trust me a bit here.

I am going to say something that might make some of you throw this book in the trash can and run the other direction—you might gain weight.

But also, you might not.

Or you might gain weight and then over time it will balance back out (this is what happened for me).

A significant turning point in my relationship with food and body was when I said, "fuck it. If I have to gain some weight to finally get over all this, I will." I was so tired of it. Tired of doing the same things every single day. Tired of thinking the same thoughts every single day. Tired of having my head in a toilet. Tired of eating. Tired of weighing. Tired of the constant stream of anxiety and chatter about carbs, calories, and how my stomach looked.

When I stopped living in fear of gaining weight, that was when things turned for me. Probably like you, I lived in the "I'm terrified I'll gain five hundred pounds and never exercise again and only eat pizza and donuts for the rest of my life if I don't obsess!" mindset.

And it never happened.

Part of this work involves a little blind faith that exactly what you want CAN happen.

Because, if you are here and reading this, I'm going to assume you have tried a lot of ways to figure out this food thing.

So try something new.

Because when you try something new, you can get a new result.

Legalization helps you establish trust between yourself and food again. Real trust.

For almost six months, I ate ice cream every single night and cereal every single morning. Those were two of my biggest binge foods. It's still a little mind-blowing that I can now keep multiple boxes of cereal in my house and several containers of ice cream in the freezer and completely forget about them. I can do that because I no longer *needed* those things. Ice cream still sounded good but I didn't want it in the way I did before. I didn't *have* to have it. It wasn't like this force making me eat it. I had a choice. I had a choice because of the allowance I had given myself with food. I didn't fear never getting it again. I knew that if in an hour, or tomorrow, or next week I wanted some, I would have some.

By freely allowing myself to eat it, and eat it whenever I wanted, the shininess wore off. It wasn't that I started hating ice cream; now I could consciously decide if I wanted it or not. I had some space between the thought and the action.

Many people want to skip this phase in figuring out their food stuff, which is understandable! And it is a phase. It isn't something you have to keep doing, it isn't something that lasts forever. It is kind of like a skill, or like riding a bike.

I know, the most overused analogy, but just go with it.

When you are learning to ride a bike, you have training wheels. And eventually, your parents take them off for you and you ride without them. A year later, if you crash the bike, you don't think, "I have to go back to training wheels all over again and relearn how to ride my bike."

If you crash your bike, you realize you can't take curbs the way you thought, or you need to lean a little less when turning. You don't go back to training wheels. You've moved past that.

As I mentioned, it can feel scary! Especially if you are someone that wants to lose weight or doesn't like their body. Letting yourself eat carby, sugary things is counterintuitive to everything you want! But by doing this part, you reach the level of freedom and peace you have been after with all those other plans.

You know that you can live in a house with a box of Oreos and not have them calling your name until you polish them off.

You can keep chocolate in your cupboard and forget about it until you crave it.

You can think brownies sound good and eat one . . . or not! Either way, it's not a big deal.

Really quick, I want to clarify this point though, because this is a part you might get hung up on.

You won't reach a day where you *never* want donuts, chocolate, chips, or Red Vines again.

You may have thought or even been taught that if you just let yourself eat all the things, eventually you reach a day when you never want it again.

I've eaten *so much* cookie dough. I mean, so much. Straight outta the Pillsbury tube. So much I felt sick. And I still wanted more days, weeks, or months later.

Where you DO get to, is a point where you can choose.

The newness and excitement of the food you spent years restricting wears off, and you can have a choice around what you eat, when, and how. It isn't a fight, it isn't a struggle, it isn't an exhausting decision. It's as boring as your relationship to water, "Do I want some water right now?"

When you know you can have a particular food any time you want, you have the ability to decide whether you really want it at that moment or not.

You get to have a choice.

Let me share an example. For a few months, my client came to our sessions telling me all she wanted was carbs. She was feeling better around food as a whole but couldn't stop fearing that she would never want vegetables or salads again. When you are going through this, a few months feels like ETERNITY. But this woman had been struggling with bingeing and bulimia for decades. This process of creating concrete trust with food was where her work was. It was why she kept struggling.

And during our work together, the change happened.

"Last night, I made some roasted veggies and a salad to go with dinner."

The change was happening and she didn't see it.

"You remember when you thought something like this could neverrrrr happen? You thought you would just want french fries forever."

She laughed. "Yes! And I didn't even realize I was doing this. I do want to eat vegetables now. I genuinely want salad again and not because it's low calorie or healthier but because I actually enjoy the taste of it."

BUT WHAT ABOUT EMOTIONAL EATING?

"Intuitive eating isn't working for me! I am still stress-eating potato chips like a maniac!" Intuitive eating helps you get back in touch with your body. It does not resolve emotional eating.

Intuitive eating fails you for two reasons:

One: You turn it into another diet. Not consciously, but you are so programmed to make everything a diet or set of right and wrong rules, it happens without you even knowing.

Two: You think all your emotional eating problems will now be gone, and when everything isn't resolved, you assume intuitive eating is another diet or program that failed you. Or that you failed. So you find another diet.

Right now, you need to focus on paying attention to your body. Maybe you follow your body's directions, maybe you don't; just start paying attention. Without judgment!

When you leave years or decades of dieting and abusing your body, give yourself the opportunity to rediscover what YOU want as opposed to what society and diet culture tells you that you should want. Ask yourself these questions:

Is this physical hunger or emotional hunger? How did that dinner sit in my stomach?

How am I feeling?

What sounds good?

SUGAR

"I am addicted to sugar." No, you're not.

We can't talk about legalization without talking about sugar. We can't really talk about food and feeling out of control around food without talking about sugar.

A lot of my clients say the same thing, "Once I start, I just can't stop," "I think I am addicted to sugar," or something to that extent. I get it, but I think other things could be going on.

I went to Overeaters Anonymous meetings and Food Addict meetings for years to try and get ahold of my eating. I believed that "once I start, I just can't stop," and I had YEARS of evidence to back that up.

But I didn't know the things I have already taught you about. All the previous items I've covered lay the foundation for you to not feel out of control around sugar.

A huge reason people feel "addicted" to sugar is because they are eating it on its own.

What I mean by that is . . . If you have a donut at 7:00 a.m. on an empty stomach with a cup of coffee, that is going to physically feel significantly different from a donut at 10:00 a.m. after you've had some eggs, sausage, and hashbrowns for breakfast.

This is because the donut at 7:00 a.m. is immediately spiking your blood sugar, then dropping it just as quickly. Then you feel tired and hungry and want something to spike it again. When you have the donut at 10:00 a.m. after a meal, you have some other nutrients inside you to balance out your blood sugar.

Most people don't feel great eating a bunch of sugar on an empty stomach because of the impact it has on your blood sugar. What you eat *with*, or before, your sugar matters.

So eat the donut, but have it with some protein and fat too.

If you want to experiment with sweet treats or any other foods that used to be off-limits, actually take the time to enjoy it. Especially with sugar. It's normal to want to hide out, not let anyone see you, and sneak the food.

But we aren't doing that anymore. :)

I love to tell my ladies, "If you eat it, own it!"

If you want a bowl of Cinnamon Toast Crunch after dinner, own that shit! Put it in a bowl, pull up a chair, and chow down.

Women who've been trapped in the cycle of dieting often devour their food at lightning speed, barely pausing to taste what's on their plates. For them, eating isn't an experience—it's a chore to rush through, or something done in secret, away from prying eyes.

When you wolf down your meals that way, achieving any genuine satisfaction becomes an insurmountable challenge—it's practically impossible!

Take the time to enjoy it. Sit down.

Put it on a plate. Taste it. Savor it.

EAT YOUR DAMN LUNCH!

Not just lunch but ALL meals.

Lunch is the meal I always hear people skip, or they say, "I only had time for a few bites!"

If you are anything like ninety-seven percent of the clients I work with, you either A: Never actually have a meal. You snack, graze, and pick at food all day long. Maybe you think it's saving you in calories, maybe you think "once I start eating I just can't stop," maybe you "just don't have the time," or it could be something else. But you ain't eatin' a meal!

B: If you have a meal, it's at your desk. You're inhaling a burrito with one hand and typing with the other, with an open bag of chips, and you're surprised to reach your hand in the bag again and notice you ate the whole damn bag!

You rarely take the time to sit down, prepare, enjoy, and savor a meal. Taking time to prioritize meals is huge in this work. If you have a history of dieting you likely have a history of grazing all day or trying to not eat for as long as possible. And then, when night falls (more on nighttime eating later), you feel out of control and like your stomach is a bottomless pit, and you go to bed stuffed and feeling sick. Then you use that as proof and say, "I am out of control around food. So tomorrow, I am going to buckle down. I am planning and preparing even better. I am NOT going through what I just went through!" And when you wake in the morning, you are right back to restricting, and the cycle begins again.

To break that cycle, prioritize meals.

I suggest *at least* three full, satisfying, delicious meals a day and probably a snack or two. But three meals minimum to get started. "But I am never hungry in the morning." Are you never hungry in the morning because you binge in the evening and are still full in the morning? When you skip breakfast or eating for half of the day, it isn't uncommon for you to get *really* hungry in the evening. It isn't that anything is wrong with you, it is just that you literally didn't eat anything, or barely anything, all day long, so you'd better believe your body is going to be like "FEED ME!"

There is nothing wrong with snacking, and the longer you do this work, I PROMISE the more trust you will have with your body and food. Snacking for most people just isn't very satisfying. And it can be annoying to feel like you are never not eating. You eat something, then forty-five minutes later, you are hungry again; it can get distracting. A good way to gauge how satisfying your meals are is to see how long it takes you to get hungry.

I know if I just have a chicken Caesar salad for lunch, I am going to be hungry in about an hour to ninety minutes. That just isn't enough food for me. But if I had a chicken Caesar, a roll with butter, and a cup of chili, that would probably last me a bit longer. I probably wouldn't feel hungry for several hours after that.

When you begin this work, start by simply taking inventory of what's going on. It is easy to jump on the shame train, and let me tell ya, that is going nowhere fast. If you have a morning where all you had were oats for breakfast and forty-five minutes later you are hungry, instead of going down the "OMG! What is wrong with me. I am always hungry and never stop eating" spiral, be more curious. Like, "Hmm. Okay. It doesn't seem like oats are cutting it anymore. Maybe I need to add in a couple of hard-boiled eggs and some bacon. Let's see if that makes a difference in how I feel."

Consider this to be more like a science experiment rather than a test that is pass-fail.

If you've been on the diet/binge, eat everything/eat nothing, doing really good/doing really bad rollercoaster, we have to start getting your body used to adequate amounts of food coming in consistently, we have to start recreating that trust with yourself. And it will take a little practice which is why you have to think of this as an experiment or more of a phase of observation and not as something that will be permanent.

EATING IS EMOTIONAL

Here's the truth. No one is eating dessert after a full meal because they are "hungry." They want dessert because they desire a variety of tastes, flavors, and textures swirling around in their mouth.

And there is nothing wrong with that!

Food is pleasurable.

Let me say that again: IT IS OKAY TO EAT FOR PLEASURE.

The biggest problem I see with people who want something sweet after a meal is the idea that this is a problem. Because when you think what you are doing is a problem, what happens?

You get super weird!

You feel tense, you hide, or you panic.

Instead of trying to fight the urge only to find yourself eating it anyway but not even getting to enjoy it because the layer of guilt is spread so thick . . . just eat it. Without guilt.

And enjoy it.

Order something that genuinely sounds tasty (including dessert!). I can't tell you the number of times I would make myself a big-ass salad for lunch and then twenty minutes later be rummaging around in the kitchen looking for just a liiiiittle something else.

Veggies, heads of broccoli, boatloads of baby carrots—they will fill you up, but they won't satisfy you.

I want you to feel satisfied. Because, we will get to this in a little bit, but this is so much deeper than just the food you're eating; it is about allowing yourself to chill out and enjoy life.

My client Katie experienced this:

I ordered exactly what I wanted at breakfast. I didn't sub out egg whites or get the healthiest thing on the menu, I got exactly what I wanted and ate until I was satisfied, which, shockingly, wasn't the whole plate and then some. What was even more shocking though, was I wasn't snacking an hour after I left the restaurant. I was able to go about my day and thoughts of food or fixating on my next meal were nowhere to be found. I just got to live my life without all that noise for the first time in a long time. I can't believe how much brain space thinking about food took up before!

Try This: Finding Food Satisfaction

Here are my top four tips for moving toward physical and mental satisfaction around food.

1. Set aside time to eat. If you are one of those people who works through her lunch break, I am challenging you to set a timer and take a legitimate lunch and eat a legitimate meal.

2. Sit down and eat. Put it on a plate. Taste it. Savor it. I recommend the first few times or few weeks you try to limit distractions, especially if you are out of touch with what real hunger and fullness feels like. It is harder to notice your hunger and fullness cues when you are distracted. This isn't something you have to do forever. We all have days where we have no choice but to cram an Eggo waffle or turkey sandwich in our mouth hole while doing three other things. Especially in the beginning while you are laying the foundation for a new relationship with food, try to carve out some time to eat and enjoy your food.

3. Eat food you genuinely enjoy. This seems like a no-brainer, but many of you are running on diet brain decisions. This doesn't mean you have to go out tomorrow and eat all the pizza, fried chicken, and ice cream. Just start asking yourself, "What really sounds good? What do I want to eat?"

4. Eat full meals. If you are hungry forty-five minutes after a meal, it is a good indicator that it wasn't enough food. A hearty meal should last you around three or four hours.

CHAPTER 12:
BODY IMAGE

Right now, if I had to guess, I'd say it feels like your mind and your body are completely detached, separate entities. You might hear yourself saying, "I know what to do but can't seem to do it!" Or, "I am not even hungry and I keep eating!" You eat when you're stuffed and don't eat when you're hungry; you push yourself when you're exhausted and do nothing on days when you know a little movement would help.

We are going to start closing that gap and get your brain and body on the same team—because they are both you.

If you're anything like me and the women I work with, for years you've probably treated your body like it's a problem to be solved. You speak to it horribly, you think mean things about it, and you do not have a compassionate, understanding relationship with it.

Establishing a functioning and solid relationship with your body is going to be important not only with food but just in LIFE! Many women I've worked with constantly second-guess themselves. They're always spinning in indecision. Anytime they choose something—anything—they fear it's wrong. They wait for the other shoe to drop. They have to ask twenty-seven other people what they think they should do. This indicates that your relationship with yourself is strained, which is a direct result of dieting and or trying to change your body motivated by hate.

Your relationship with your body is just like a relationship you have with anyone else. The kinder you are, the more you show up for the person and support them, oftentimes the better and closer the relationship gets. But diet culture and the society we live in constantly sends messages like, "No pain, no gain!" Or, "Sweat is fat crying!" Or, "No days off!" The constant going, doing, hustling, and grinding is applauded—all the while you move further and further from yourself.

You may get more and more attention, compliments, and questions like, "Can you help me with my willpower too?"—and that is truly the massive fuckery about all of this. Eating disorders and disordered eating are widely referred to as "fitness routines." So many of the "What I ate in a day" articles display what I would consider to be a strained relationship with food. I'm saying this because the war you're fighting with your body isn't your fault. But it is now your responsibility to see through all that bullshit and do something different.

The more you immerse yourself in this work, the sharper your ability becomes to spot the lies embedded in diet culture. It's natural to feel a surge of anger initially; believe me, I've been there! And trust me, that anger is justified. Dieting, body shaming, obsessing over food, and never feeling thin, strong, or toned enough stole precious years from my life. Years I wasted on a treadmill, meticulously weighing chicken, when I could have been truly living. Years I spent fixated on macros and the numbers on a scale, instead of engaging in activities that genuinely sparked joy.

So, if you find yourself simmering with anger over the next few months as you begin to realize just how pervasive diet culture is, know that I understand completely. Your anger is not only valid; it's necessary.

STOP TRYING TO LOVE YOUR BODY

The biggest mistake I see women make?

Trying to go from "I'm a disgusting mess that needs to get her life together immediately!" to " I love myself! I think I am beautiful. I love my body."

OOOOOOH LORD, THAT'S A BIG JUMP!

This whole "love yourself" idea is great and all, and may be a long—LONG—term goal, but for right now, we all just need to relax a little around it. In fact, trying to love your body may be the thing that will keep you from ever liking it.

Why?

Because it is such an aggressive shift. Let me give you an example.

Let's say you are single. You go on a date. But before you go on the date, someone tells you that you *must* fall in love with this person *today*, and that you are moving in with them tomorrow.

The guy was fine and all, the date went okay, he was kind of cute, but DAMN! The pressure to love him just like that . . . it's so strong that you panic and run.

He may have been someone you could have fallen in love with, but because the pressure was so front-loaded, you bailed!

See what I'm saying?

If you think you're gross, hate a certain body part, or desperately want to look differently, jumping to love will be fake.

Think about some of your best relationships, maybe with a friend, maybe your partner or parents. They take time, attention, and nurturing. Imagine talking to your mom (or daughter or pet) the way you speak to yourself. You wouldn't! And if you did, they probably wouldn't want to spend time around you. Odds are, any amazing relationship you have in your life took work and attention to get to that place. It took understanding and compassion.

I honestly thought I'd cross a checkpoint in my life where I would have done enough work and I'd never think badly about my body again. I believed once I stopped binge eating and purging, my entire life would change! I would never have another negative thought about myself.

Spoiler alert: that didn't happen.

This meant every time I *did* have a negative body image day, I interpreted it to mean I had failed. And since I failed, I might as well binge. This is a good example of all-or-nothing thinking.

Body image work is more complex than the food stuff. Body image work really boils down to self-acceptance. No one cares about their food if they aren't even more concerned with how their body looks. To end the war with food and regain trust with yourself, body image work is critical.

For many, what started this whole thing years ago was hating your body: wanting to lose just a few pounds, wanting to tone up, giving the grapefruit diet a try . . . And it probably worked in the beginning, most things do for a little while, and ever since then, you've been chasing that dragon only to end up further and further away from your goal. You will do body image and body acceptance work for your whole life because we continually grow, change, evolve, and age, and with that comes the continual need to accept our own bodies. It will not be the way it is right now. It will be so much more calm and smooth and less aggressive.

If not loving . . . then what?

Accepting.

Acknowledging.

ACCEPT–LIKE–LOVE

Body acceptance simply means accepting, "This is my body." You don't have to love it right now; you don't even have to like it. All I'm asking is that you focus on moving toward acceptance.

To go from hating your body to loving it in one leap isn't very realistic. One way to start building a better body image is to practice with "bridge thoughts." Bridge thoughts are small steps in the direction we ultimately want to go. So if you are currently at the place of "I hate my body," a bridge thought for you could be "This is my body." If you hate your stomach currently, you could start with "This is my stomach."

You can use bridge thoughts to work on changing your beliefs in any area of your life. While you do so, prepare for your old thoughts to pop up often. You've had a lifetime of practice thinking the old thoughts; you won't get rid of them so easily. This is why it's important to dedicate time to come up with new thoughts, so the moment the old thoughts come up, the new ones are in the front of your brain, ready to replace them.

I often tell clients it will feel like you have two personalities: Current You and Future You. Future You needs to redirect Current You, to let you know, "Hey, I hear you, but I got it. I'll take it from here."

It's not going to be easy, so I want you to burn into your brain this truth: accepting your body does not mean you are giving up on life; it does not mean you will never stop eating, never stop gaining weight; it doesn't mean your life is over; and it definitely doesn't mean you will die a sad, lonely death.

Body acceptance means you accept your damn body!

It means you stop waking up pissed at yourself for existing, and you start accepting it.

Resisting and fighting reality is exhausting, not to mention we never win.

My rain example illustrates this beautifully.

I hate rain. I want sunshine 365, baby! But I've always lived in places where it gets gray and damp. On rainy days, I could look out my window and be livid. I could run outside and scream and stomp and demand it stop raining, but the rain doesn't give a shit. The rain is just gonna keep pouring, and I'm going to be exhausted and even angrier.

This is an example of resistance.

Alternatively, I could look out my window, see the rain, be kinda bummed—maybe have to rearrange my afternoon plans—but decide to cozy up on the couch and watch a movie or read a book. I still hate the rain, but instead of resisting it, I'm working with it. I am still not excited about water falling from the sky, but I'm not fighting it.

As we do this for longer and start really seeing our body for what it is and all it can do, we can start appreciating it more.

It may seem impossible, but let me share with you the process my client Meg went through:

Meg had done a bodybuilding competition about a year and a half before we worked together. In true binge-eater fashion, she went all in. She hired the trainer, she got the nutritionist, she tracked, weighed, and measured. She had completely transformed her body into something it had never been before. She pushed it, starved it, dehydrated it, and she got shredded!

Cool cool cool . . . And then!

She gained weight. She was exhausted. She couldn't look at another chicken breast. She was burned-out. And she was terrified of exercise because all she knew was "GO HARD OR GO HOME! IF IT ISN'T AN HOUR, IT ISN'T WORTH IT! THE ONLY

REASON TO WORK OUT IS TO CHANGE HOW YOUR BODY LOOKS!"

Throughout our work, we started to create a new relationship to her body. One that wasn't abusive, one that wasn't extreme. And she had the same fears every client does. "If I am not pushing, forcing, or fixating, I will never stop eating and never stop gaining weight." The desire to fix your body will be strong. You have been taught and conditioned to think this. And it can one thousand percent change.

Early on, Meg wasn't sure she would ever be able to look at this new body in the mirror with anything other than disgust. But a few months into our work together, she sent me a message:

"I had just gotten out of the shower, and I got a glimpse of my body in the mirror and I . . . I actually thought I looked sexy! I never thought I could like 'this' body, but I think I am finally starting to!"

Over the months, we had cleaned her social media and her brain of all the bullshit body image pictures that were making her feel like garbage. We worked on simply acknowledging and accepting her body. Like, she actually looked at herself in the mirror and practiced not tearing it to shreds.

And with that work and effort, she moved into a space of truly appreciating what her body was not.

Part of the work I did with Meg and with all my clients is "Desensitization." We have to get you used to looking at your current body. Not what you think you look like in your head, not what you look like in photos, not what you are seeing online, but your actual body in its truest form.

Why is this important?

Let's say you haven't seen a friend in a year. You only have memories of her.

You finally get together in real life, and you are in SHOCK!

Her hair is black and has a pixie cut! It was shoulder length and blond the last time you saw her. Not only that, but her eyebrows are darker and she is wearing lipstick. *Who is this person?* The thing is, she has had this look for over a year. None of her other friends are shocked by it, so why are you? Because you haven't seen her. At this point, none of her other friends can even imagine her with blond hair again, the black hair is just so fitting for her. Why? Because they are used to it.

If you never look at your body, you will be shocked when you see it.

Try This: Bridge Thoughts and Desensitization

Bridge Thoughts

Set a timer for one minute and write down things you don't like about your body or thoughts that usually pop into your head when you think about yourself. When the minute is up, go back through the list. For each habitual thought you've written, cross it out and write next to it a more neutral bridge thought that will move you gently toward acceptance. Keep this list handy in your phone if you need to.

Desensitization

Look at yourself in the mirror. For fifteen seconds, sixty seconds, I don't care, just start. Just start looking at yourself.

Personally, I like to do this naked because I actually feel the most attractive in my rawest form, but that may be *way* too far for you. So just start with what you are comfortable with.

Then, move into some acceptance. Say, "So this is what my ol' meat sack looks like, eh? Okay. Well. I don't love it, but here we are." Or "This is my body." Something super basic and nonemotional.

As you keep doing this and sheer acceptance starts to feel pretty comfortable, look for something you like. "My shoulders look so good!" "My thighs look so strong in this skirt." "I love how my back looks." "I love the way my skin looks so soft." Something.

You don't have to spend hours doing this, and honestly I think that does more harm than good. Because all that is doing is placing more focus and importance on your appearance, which no one needs. Life is a hell of a lot more than what your body looks like.

Remember, when we change pretty much anything, but especially our thoughts, it doesn't happen overnight. You must intentionally practice the new thoughts. Your intentional thoughts right now are likely not serving you but they happen fast and without any effort. They are just there: a habit. Your job is to decide to *intentionally* feed yourself new thoughts, or your current thoughts will continue to dominate.

CHAPTER 13:
DOING THINGS DIFFERENTLY

We're circling back because I think you might need a reminder about now: change feels hard because it feels wrong.

You have conditioned yourself—or maybe been conditioned—to live a certain way and believe certain things. The beliefs are so deeply ingrained in you now that *not* doing them feels like someone is asking you to run red lights. You see the red light ahead and think, "There is no way I'm just blowing right through that! That is crazy talk." You don't want to die.

This is how change feels—except you aren't going to die. Not even close.

It turns out I am really big on analogies, which I didn't realize until recently. So I'm going to share another example I once gave my client Kate. She found it helpful, so I hope you do too.

Right now in your brain, you have this pathway formed. It is beautiful. It's a paved path with hanging flower baskets and cute lights, and after half a mile there are water fountains. The path is straight, easy to follow, and an enjoyable walk. But every time you get to the end of it, the end of this path you've created, you have to jump into a fiery pit of lava—your own choice. But, because this is just an imaginary path, you can come back to life and start over. But that's the thing! You just start over. You keep doing the same thing over and over because the path is so beautiful, easy, and tempting in the beginning. But this beautiful path keeps you stuck. You never move forward because that beautiful damn path always ends in a fiery death.

There is another path though. This one is densely packed, like you'd find in the jungle, choked with vines, trees, bugs, and you can't see ten feet in front of you. You have no idea where this path goes. It looks terrifying. But there is also a machete at your feet. For years, you've taken the paved path with flower baskets for obvious reasons—only to end up exactly where you started.

You now have to make a choice. Do you keep going down the paved path that leads to certain death? Or do you choose the one that looks impossible to get through, where you have no idea what to expect, but where there is also hope and possible healing?

You say, "Fuck this."

Because something great always comes along after someone reaches the point of "fuck this."

THE ONE THING

People will ask me, "What changed? What was that major pivot? What was the *one thing* that shifted for you?" I have thought a lot about this answer. It isn't exciting.

I wanted better. I wanted a better life in a calm and focused way. I felt manic during attempts at finding my career and trying to crack the code on my food. I felt desperate. I got to a place of, "Okay. This is where I am. And now I want better."

I could have kept living with daily binges. I could have kept living with massive amounts of anxiety, wondering if people really liked me or just said that and internally wanted me to leave. I could have carried on. I didn't want to. I wanted a different life, a different way of being, and I wanted it one percent more than I wanted to carry on.

Many people think they need to be one hundred percent ready for the change. They need to feel it with every ounce of their body, but that was never the case for me. I loved drinking. I loved the feeling of it. I loved escaping life. I loved the freedom of completely zoning out while I mindlessly crammed a yellow cake with vanilla frosting and brightly colored roses into my mouth. I loved the intense energy hit I got while bingeing. I loved feeling like I had this protective shield around me. I loved how bingeing, or alcohol, or distancing myself from others made me feel like I had the upper hand. Like, "You can't hurt me."

Until it didn't.

Until I wanted something different. When I thought about my life five or ten years in the future, I didn't want that baggage. I didn't want those behaviors. You don't have to be one hundred percent ready for change—and you don't have to have a good reason for wanting it.

You know what kept me going to AA meetings in the beginning? Hot dudes. Which, by the way, looking back, I have to wonder if there wasn't still a lot of alcohol in my system like a year after I stopped drinking, because those dudes were *not* hot!

In all seriousness, when we change, when we act in alignment with who we want to be and the life we want to have, our standards change. I used to settle for all kinds of bullshit because I hated who I was. I didn't feel deserving of good things. I felt like a fraud. But slowly, with each layer of work I did, each behavior

I changed, each way of living I looked at, I started wanting different things in my life. I wanted different people in my sphere. I set different goals for myself.

When I got sober, everything was different. I had no clue what to do. No idea what to do with my hands. Who to hang out with. What to say when I went to parties. Then I found myself spending time with other people who didn't know what to do and how to behave. People who didn't want to spend six hours on a Friday night getting hammered and then all day Saturday recovering. I started spending time with people who went for walks and climbed mountains and had hobbies other than drinking.

When I stopped obsessing about food and my body, that was an even bigger identity shift because, as you've read, food was my first "thing." I don't want to call it my first addiction because I really wasn't addicted to food in the way I thought I was, but for lack of a better word and because it communicates clearly how I felt, I will use it.

Food. Restriction. Binge eating. Exercise. Calories. All of it. It was my first tool to manage life. Without this "addiction" occupying ninety-five percent of my head space, I had no CLUE who I was. I realized I could see this in one of two different ways:

One: I am now a lost soul with no direction.

Or two: I finally get to live the life and become the person I've always wanted to be.

I see people struggle with this sense of failure when they change. As if there's an unwritten rule (or maybe it was literally written down in your household) to stay the same. To keep the same job and relationships, eat the same foods, do the same hobbies, and just be happy forever.

Well, there is one huge problem with that: we evolve. All those things are not set in stone; they're scratched in sand. And it is a beautiful thing because it means you can CHANGE YOUR MIND!

You aren't a failure or a fuckup because you made a major career change in your fifties. You aren't destined to be alone forever if you end a relationship in your late thirties. You get to change your mind. When you embrace that notion, a new layer of life begins. Because when you don't believe it's true that we can change our minds, that nothing is truly fixed, every single decision feels like life or death.

As I'm typing these words in my office, I'm living in Indiana. INDIANA! Never ever in my life did I imagine I would be here, nor did I ever want to be, and yet—here I am!

I tend to sprint more toward the side of completely fucking wild as opposed to being calm, cool, and collected. I will admit, I am not the most chill person you will ever meet. I want a plan. I want to know what is going on. And I want to be in control. :)

So when I was deciding whether I wanted to move to Indiana while we were in the process of selling and packing up my childhood home, and I was finding someone to take over the gym my dad and I had opened, I felt a sense of failure. I also felt fear. What if this was the wrong choice? What if I hate it? What if the gym gets huge and I could have been successful here? What if something happens to my dad and I'm not here to help? What if, what if, what if! That is a familiar response to a problem for me, which as you can probably tell, is not too effective. It usually leads to a complete meltdown and, of course, eating all the food.

"If I hate it, I can leave. This isn't forever." I had to tell myself that on repeat.

And even that didn't stop the meltdowns because having emotions is part of the human experience. We spend so much time trying to be less of this, more of that, and I say run headfirst into all of it. Cry. Yell. Dance. Scream. Be excited. Feel terrified. Admit to not knowing. It is all okay.

And that is what changed.

I started letting myself be me.

I stopped trying to be the perfect human with the perfect body and the perfect relationship to food and have the perfect life and make all the perfect decisions, and I got better at doing life on life's terms.

I stopped trying to control every single thing.

THE RULES AREN'T REAL

You live in your own personal glass box. A glass box that you cannot see, nor are you aware of it even containing you, but it does. You were born into this box, and it has been strengthened over the years. It got stronger through school, through peers, through education, through your experiences, through media, and through your culture.

But it is glass. And once you recognize you are in it, you can break out.

So much of your suffering comes from trying to be happy in that box, but you, my friend, do not belong in a box. What you want for yourself cannot be shoved, morphed, and manipulated into some box so that society can bop you on the head with a tiny magic wand and say, "I announce that you are a good girl."

No.

Hell no.

Pretending to be content in that box is a slow and painful death.

Remember when I mentioned the time when I was a nursing assistant and living life the "right" way, but was miserable? I was in the box. I was in a box that I had to break my legs to fit into, but by god I did it. I finally had that "looks good, fits in" vibe that I'd wanted my entire life.

Until I realized I hated it.

I realized I needed to stretch. To breathe.

To move.

To be me.

I didn't realize I was in the box until I found myself outside looking in.

It's very normal and very human to want to be loved and accepted. That's what most of us want, but what is the true cost?

When you were younger, you may have been willing to just go with the flow in certain situations. You may have been able to quiet the screams from your body as it pleaded for food or rest, but at what cost? If you get the body, the job, the house, and the life that most would drool over but it costs you your sanity—is it worth it?

Maybe it is.

Or maybe it used to be, but you can't pretend any longer.

The thing about this glass box that you put yourself in is that you do it to make yourself appear a certain way to other people. Think about this for a second: if you were on a deserted island and you weren't fearing for your life or anything, you were just hanging out for a couple months, how would you feel about your body? You probably wouldn't give two shits.

You care because you care about what others think. You spend your whole life going and doing and being so "they" will like you. "They" will approve. "They" will accept you.

Do you even know who they are?

For most of us, there are about three people we immediately think of when we think of "they" (closest family and friends); the rest are kind of make-believe people. You aren't even sure who "they" are but you know they're scrutinizing what you do with your life.

I have a real tough-love statement here: nobody cares. Yikes . . . I'll let that settle for a second. Let's try again. Nobody cares.

Everyone is running around thinking about themselves. And if they do care about us, it's for about five minutes and then they forget and go back to thinking about *their* life, because that is what we do.

The people that are worth the time of day don't give two shits about your stomach rolls or if you take a different job.

Break out of your own glass box.

Another harsh truth is: some people may be disappointed when you change. They liked you better when you were living life the way they felt most comfortable with. They liked you safe and contained in the box. The good news is, that isn't your problem to deal with. You can live your entire life trying to be enough in someone else's eyes, or you can start being enough for YOU.

You can start showing up for yourself in such a way that when you lay your head down at night you think, "Damn . . . I'm doing it, aren't I." You can start living in a way that makes YOU proud because you are the most important person you live for.

This might mean you decide to stop putting off your workouts, or maybe you'll do the workout but give yourself permission to quit early if need be.

Maybe it means spending a little extra money to get the meal delivery service because the peace of mind it brings you is priceless. Perhaps it looks like ending a relationship that's long overdue. Or making a move you've wanted for years but been terrified to execute. Or leaving a job that makes you hate your life. Or simply never settling for a pair of jeans that don't make you feel like a 10/10.

Every "should" that comes out of your mouth— question it. Is it something you actually want, or are you trying to force yourself back into the box? You have to clear out the old you to make room for the new.

REST

The shoulds might be particularly loud any time you make time to rest. But it's not rest if you beat yourself up about it the whole time.

Resting never comes without guilt. So much worth is tied to *what* you do. How much is accomplished. How productive you are. How busy you are.

Saying yes to others happens in the blink of an eye, but taking a weekend off without checking your damn work phone is nearly impossible. We believe if it isn't hard, if it doesn't hurt, we're not pushing enough. And the world is grooming you for this.

Open up Instagram for twelve seconds and you can't escape someone telling you to just want it more.

Try harder. No days off.

No pain no gain.

You are endlessly sold messages that if you aren't pushing yourself to the max every day, you don't deserve whatever it is you're after. While you are resting, your competition is working. And that, my friend, is how many a fucked-up relationship to food and body begins.

Here's what I've found to be true for myself and the women I've worked with: it doesn't have to hurt to move us forward.

Just because you don't go one hundred percent on the daily, just because you aren't aggressively fixated on something, it doesn't mean you will never do hard things or make progress.

I want to be sure you hear this, because I personally felt like if I wasn't killing myself, obsessing over food, weight, my bank account, or worrying about *something*, I would literally do nothing and just die.

No.

If you're an all-or-nothing thinker, your mind might go there.

"Well, if I'm not eating healthy, I'm eating pizza and donuts literally 24/7."

"If I'm not killing myself in the workouts, I will never get stronger and achieve the body I want."

"If I am not constantly worrying about it, it will never get done."

This is the hustle mentality.

And listen, I love me some hustle and hard work. But one feels terrible and one feels rewarding.

This is what I lived and breathed and what, ultimately, made me miserable. I didn't think I was worthy if I wasn't always busting my ass in some way. Excuse me, let me rewrite that: in some *productive* way. If I wasn't burning calories, meal prepping, excelling in a career, I was falling off track. And that was my life.

I was terrified to trust myself. I was terrified to loosen my grip on control. I was terrified to be me *because* I had no trust in myself. But as I loosened my grip on food and discovered I actually could stop eating or gaining weight, I gained a little more trust with myself.

I kept going and doing because I feared losing momentum. I feared getting so lax and lazy I would just decide to never do anything ever again. Letting life be easy was ironically the hardest thing I had ever done. It's this fear that keeps women in the cycle of dieting, bingeing, and burning the candle at both ends. It is safe to relax.

It is safe to relax.

It is safe to relax.

I know the word "trauma" gets thrown around all the time these days, but I truly believe women with a history of bingeing, dieting, and disordered eating have trauma around food and exercise. You are repairing years and years of trauma.

Mentally I know you're raring to go, ready for more, and I love that about you so much—but I want you to think of this work as a major surgery. When you go in for back surgery, after a few weeks you may be itching to push yourself. Mentally, you're tired of sitting on your ass, but physically, you know you can't get up and run around. Your doctor told you to recover in the best way possible; you need to rest right now. It's annoying because you want to be living life! But the better you treat your recovery post-surgery, the sooner you can get back to enjoying life.

Resting. Relaxing. Eating more. Sleeping more. Doing less. Like, way less. It may feel gluttonous, it may feel weak, it may feel terrifying . . . and it may also feel like a huge relief. What you need to do for yourself now, this month, this year, is not what you will need to do in the future. The way you live your life two months after surgery isn't how you will live two years after surgery.

If you are naturally more of a busy person and you really don't want to lounge or relax, own that! I tend to be a little more that way and this was something I felt bad about. I thought I needed to be SUPER chill and never have too much going on at once, and well, that isn't my personality and frankly that just isn't the way life works for most of us. But this also falls into some all-or-nothing thinking, big surprise. Those times when you read a book or article, see a comment on a post, or get feedback from a family member and think, "Okay! I am going super Zen mode! I am going to be one hundred percent intentional with every yes I give, with all my free time, and with the tasks I pick up."

This will last for approximately eight minutes, and then you will be back to drowning in things to do and people to please.

Try This: The Option of Rest

Give yourself a day to respond to things.

"Hey, that sounds like fun! Let me get back to you tomorrow."

This way you don't get caught up in the excitement of doing something new or the thought of being able to help someone out, and you can consciously decide if you actually have the time and energy to take something else on.

Think of this as a process and a life change, not a check on a to-do list.

CHAPTER 14:
SELF-TRUST

Have you heard of David Goggins? He's an absolute beast! He was a Navy SEAL, completed over 60 ultra-marathons, triathlons, and ultra-triathlons. He has run on broken feet, pushed through extreme discomfort, and been told to stop countless times. He's extremely driven and passionate, and I am fascinated by him.

Note: he is horrible to follow if you're just beginning to listen to your body but good for this example.

If you're not confident in who you are, when someone like Goggins comes around in your life, you will feel like a failure. *"Should I be doing more?"* you'll wonder. *"Should I be more fit? Should I be more dedicated?"* The only one who can answer those questions is you.

There's something important we should realize about people online: we see what they want us to see. I'm not saying David Goggins is fake, not at all, but we never get the full story, so we fill in all the gaps in his life ourselves. We assume how he eats, the state of his relationships, what his house is like, or anything else in his life.

And we will compare our lives to his.

On the opposite end of the spectrum is Byron Katie. She's a speaker and author and is much softer and more lovey-dovey. She calls most of her coaching clients "honey" and talks a lot about love and caring for yourself. I think she's amazing too. The books she's written and the work she's put out into the world are incredible. I've never once heard her mention working out or say the word "fuck"—unlike Goggins who uses it as punctuation.

Neither one of these humans is better than the other. Neither is "doing it right." Both are incredible in their own way. We can learn a lot from each of them without putting them on a pedestal. It's easy to fall into the trap of wanting to *be* a person we admire—maybe you've said, at one time or another, "Oh, I wish I was *Brenda*. She is always so put together and just does it all, all of the time." But that doesn't serve us.

We don't need to become someone else. I don't need to *be* David Goggins or Byron Katie. We need to get clear on who *we* are and know when to tap into our inner Goggins or our inner Byron Katie—but then come back to ourselves and our truth.

You can admire someone without needing to be them. Which is what self-trust is all about.

Self-trust is one of my favorite topics because it's my ultimate goal for every client. When you don't trust yourself to eat, make decisions, or live your life, when you constantly crave approval from others, we never feel completely whole. Without self-trust, we never feel quite good enough.

Self-trust isn't tangible in the same way that confidence isn't tangible—meaning you can't go buy it. You don't buy the book on confidence and, *poof,* you're confident for life. It can be a fragile thing, especially in the early stages of listening to your body and changing your relationship to food. We can be susceptible to outside influences even when things are going well; when we're lacking in confidence and trust in ourselves, it's even worse.

Throughout your entire life, you'll meet people who are "better" than you and people who are "worse" than you. If you meet a thousand people, you'll encounter a thousand different opinions about life, the universe—and what *you* should do to solve your problems. Some people will tell you CrossFit is the best. Others will tell you that you should do yoga four times a week. Others will share stories about resting and reading with tea, and how that is pure bliss. Some will speak so fondly of their children; others will wish they had never conceived at all. Certain people will push you into college and a steady job; others will encourage you to go after your passions and tell you college is a waste of money.

Someone will always have an opinion on "the best way"—but remember, that's all it is. An opinion. If you don't start to become solid on who you are and what you want for yourself, in the face of all these opinions and the shiny happy people pushing them onto you, you will forever feel like you aren't doing enough, or you're doing too much, or you're just plain doing it *wrong*.

Faced with all these people who look so happy and successful, it can be difficult to resist the urge to compare ourselves. And when we finally do decide to have a go at trusting ourselves, we discover that's not all sunshine and roses either.

Self-trust can be brutal at times, and that's a conversation we are not having enough.

When we hear coaches and gurus say things like, "Be more you! Do you! Just be yourself! Trust yourself!" It sounds nice. Very motivational. Maybe you even have a Pinterest board with quotes just like that. But the truth is, self-trust can straight-up feel like shit.

When we start listening to ourselves and living our truth, other people can get hurt, which is why we people-please. It seems better to take on all the pain and suffering in our lives in order to avoid confrontation or so we don't upset anyone. This is when the eating, drinking, self-sabotaging, comes in because we create pain in ourselves to keep the peace with someone else. But when we no longer want to do that, when we no longer want to keep bending over backward for everyone else or pretending to be okay when we aren't, someone else will be disappointed.

And you know what? It sucks. Because most of us enjoy making people happy! It feels good to please others. But we reach a point where we just cannot do it anymore. The dissatisfaction gets so high that we cannot keep pretending.

So we say no. We take a different job. End the relationship. Leave a friend group. Stop showing up the way everyone has known us to show up. And it's painful.

Which is why you must lean into and onto the life you really want for yourself. You have to focus more on what you do want and less on what you don't. If you want something different, if you want to do different things, if you want to feel a different way, if you want to engage in different behaviors, you have to do things differently.

Try This: Different Choice

For the next day, *make a different choice*. Notice how I put a time stamp on that? This will help calm your anxiety so you don't slip into HOW AM I SUPPOSED TO KEEP THIS UP FOREVER!

It's one day.

Get your ass outta bed and make yourself a lavish breakfast.

Go to the event you were super stoked about but now want to bail on because you feel fat. Give yourself time to decide whether you actually want to give that person's kid a ride to the soccer game or if you need to say no.

IS IT BAD ENOUGH? AM I GOOD ENOUGH?

We're always comparing and judging; it's in our nature. It's impossible not to. We do it for safety and comfort, but oftentimes, it has the opposite effect. Comparison makes us feel silly for complaining or thinking we have a problem. It leads us to think we shouldn't be proud of our achievements because so-and-so is so much further along than we are. The possibilities for comparison-based self-sabotage are endless!

For example: My food and drinking went to the extremes. Both got so bad that the next rung on my ladder was death. While you were reading my story, you may have thought, "Dang, I have nothing to complain about. I never went through any of that."

The truth is, what I went through has nothing to do with what you're going through. There is no medal for the amount of suffering we can incur. Do not compare your life to mine or anyone else's.

Maybe you drink two glasses of wine a night to "take the edge off" or find yourself wrapped up on the couch in the dark polishing off a bag of chips. Or perhaps you have a job everyone says you are lucky to have, but you hate it. Or maybe you're in a relationship that looks good on paper but you can't shake the feeling it isn't right. If your situation feels bad to you, it is worthy of change.

Someone will always have it worse than you. Someone will always have it better.

None of that means your own pain isn't valid. I never want you to get to where I was with food and body, which is why I do what I do. I want to help you stop that juggernaut in its tracks before it mows you down, and get you on the path you want.

If your situation feels like a problem to you—it is. That's all that matters. It doesn't have to get worse and no one has to understand.

CONCLUSION:
GO LIVE YOUR BEST GODDAMN LIFE

It is real easy to get sucked into the cyclone of personal development. Why? BECAUSE IT NEVER ENDS!

A question I am routinely asked is "Can I really get over this? Will I really recover from this?"

Yes, but also, you are still going to have to exist on earth. And that is a challenge. Weight loss, body image, and "you aren't good enough" messaging is everywhere. Your weight is going to change, and how your body feels is going to change, and your mood is going to change, and nothing is constant.

So, YES, you can one hundred percent get over this "stuff," but that doesn't mean you won't still have bad days. Days you don't like your body. Weeks you wonder, "What in the actual F am I doing?" 'Cause that's life, sugar tits.

The goal isn't to achieve the perfect body, reach the land of "no bad days," and live happily ever after. That goal is going to leave you in a state of perpetual disappointment because that's not real life.

Real life is the good, bad, and the ugly.

And at a certain point, you have to decide, "This is good enough," and move the hell on with your day. Take the trip. Wear the swimsuit. Sign up for the run. Jump out of the airplane. Go to the concert in go-go boots and a sequin jumpsuit. Eat pasta at midnight. Swim naked. DO LIFE THINGS. Because those are the things that put your life into perspective. Those are the things that remind you why you are here. Those are the things that shake your life up enough to remind you that you are in fact fucking awesome and capable.

The problem with your food isn't really a problem with food; the problem is thinking you aren't good enough. That there's no way people could love you the way you are. That you have to somehow be different to be accepted.

But being you is your biggest gift.

As I write this section, I feel so much hope and excitement for you. Maybe you completely relate to my story, or maybe only a few bits and pieces felt familiar.

Either way, I hope you begin to see that your problems with food are a symptom, not a cause. And I hope you can see a way to creating the life you truly want and deserve.

As you begin moving forward, past your exhausting relationship with food and your body, the confidence you feel will ooze into all aspects of your life.

The self-doubt that felt strongest after eating in secret will no longer be there. Your confidence to speak up for what you want and need in relationships will increase.

Going after things you only ever dreamed about will actually seem kind of possible.

Because when food, body, and self-doubt have controlled your entire life, without them you will feel like an entirely new person.

Go get every single thing you want.

AFTERWORD:
FRIENDS AND FAMILY OF THOSE STRUGGLING

This is an additional note for those of you who may be reading this book and don't struggle with food, body, drinking, or an addictive personality but want to support someone who does. I know that my parents, partners, and friends all wanted to be there but had no idea how to. They had no idea what to say or what the right thing to do was. And when they would try to help, I would bite their head off.

First, the fact that you care, want to help,and want to learn, means a lot. Second, this might not be super uplifting, but this stuff is complicated! It is complicated for the person dealing with it and even more so for the person trying to offer support. Because half the time, the person directly dealing with it doesn't even know themselves what they need! So it is pretty much impossible to give someone else guidance.

Here are a few things to keep in mind.

1. Every single person is different. When I was in treatment, some of the girls loved having their family eat meals with them, others not. Some of the women wanted their partner or parents to directly ask them how they have been doing around food and body stuff, others did NOT. You have to check in with YOUR person because they may not want the kind of support the recent book you read is suggesting.

2. It's going to change. This may be frustrating to you, but it is even MORE frustrating to us. The support they want and need the first three months will not be the same during months eight through twelve, I promise that. Keep checking in, keep asking what they need, if what used to work is still helping or if things need to shift. Consider it an evolving and ongoing conversation rather than a set list of to do's. The more honest you can be, the better. Such as, "I want to support you and I am not sure how to. I don't want to feel nervous talking about this, but I do right now. I hope the more

we discuss it, the more comfortable it becomes for both of us." The more we normalize it, the easier it becomes, as opposed to this big, dark, shameful secret no one should ever know about.

3. You can't fix anyone. You can love your person. You can be there for them. You can support them. You cannot fix them or solve their problems. Please take that responsibility off yourself.

4. Shame is a core component of all of this. As I mentioned in #2, the more we can normalize it and just speak freely about it, the easier it all feels and the shame begins to evaporate. So many people struggle with food and drinking. It's actually super normal. The less shocked you can be, the less freaked out you can be, the better. Struggling with this stuff sucks and the more safe and unjudged your person can feel around you, the better.

Talk to your people, do your best, and know that you won't do it perfectly because that doesn't exist.

ABOUT THE AUTHOR

Renae Saager is a certified health and life coach and emotional eating expert who teaches go-getter women around the world how to start living a powerful, authentic life free from food and weight obsession. Tapping into her own unique journey with disordered eating and alcoholism, Renae connects with her clients on a deeper level, supporting them through the process of rewiring their brain with her no-BS approach. Renae is able to help clients challenge their mindset and begin healing, using her own sense of humor and unparalleled perspective which creates a more enjoyable and transformational process. Undoing the crazy you feel around food is Renae's specialty; the confidence and clarity gained is the guilt-free icing on the cake.

Renae works with her clients in 1:1 and small group settings, both of which are done remotely.

Interested in working together or staying in touch?
Follow me on IG: @renaesaager
Visit my website: renaesaager.com
Listen to my podcast: Ditch The Binge

BOOK SUMMARY

Welcome to *Eat Drink Think*, where the battle with food and body image ends and a life of authenticity and joy begins. Renae Saager, your guide and seasoned expert, has navigated the rough waters of disordered eating and alcoholism to discover true freedom—and she's ready to lead you to the same liberation.

This isn't just another book about eating; it's a manifesto for change, blending real-life insights with a no-BS approach and a hearty dose of humor. Renae's powerful coaching methods and personal journey inform every page, challenging you to transform your relationship with food and your body.

Eat Drink Think is more than a book; it's a movement toward living freely and fully. Renae equips you with the tools to dismantle the shackles of past food and body woes, paving the way for a future where you live boldly and eat without guilt.